DUBLIN
CITY
CENTRE
ATLAS
POCKET
EDITION

ORDNANCE
SURVEY
OF IRELAND

GW00420220

CONTENTS

CITY CENTRE TERMINUS GUIDE
LEGEND

SPECIAL THANKS TO BORD FÁILTE AND OFFICE OF PUBLIC WORKS

CITY CENTRE TERMINUS GUIDE

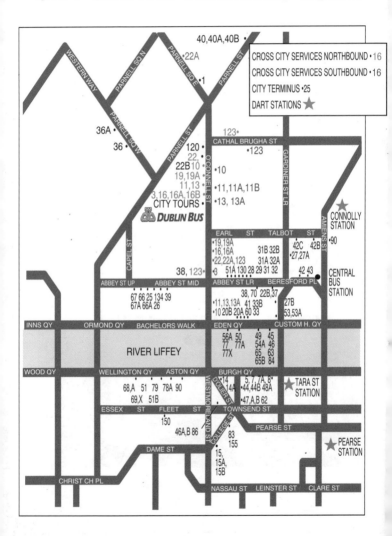

CROSS CITY SERVICES NORTHBOUND •16
CROSS CITY SERVICES SOUTHBOUND •16
CITY TERMINUS •25
DART STATIONS ★

40,40A,40B
•22A
•1
123•
36A •
36 •
120 •
22 •
22B 10
19,19A •
11,13
3,16,16A,16B
CITY TOURS •
DUBLIN BUS

CATHAL BRUGHA ST
•123
•10
•11,11A,11B
•13, 13A

CONNOLLY STATION

EARL ST   TALBOT ST
•19,19A
•16,16A   31B 32B
•22,22A,123   31A 32A
•3 51A 130 28 29 31 32

42C 42A•
•27,27A
42 43

38, 123•

CENTRAL BUS STATION

ABBEY ST UP   ABBEY ST MID   ABBEY ST LR   BERESFORD PL
67 66 25 134 39   38, 70 22B,37
67A 66A 26   •11,13,13A 41 33B   •27B
                     •10 20B 20A 60 33   53,53A

INNS QY   ORMOND QY   BACHELORS WALK   EDEN QY   CUSTOM H. QY

RIVER LIFFEY

56A 50   49 45
77 77A   54A 46
77X   65 63
            65B 84

WOOD QY   WELLINGTON QY   ASTON QY   BURGH QY
68,A 51 79 78A 90   •14   5, 7, 7A, 8•
69,X 51B   •14A   •44,44B 48A
                                 •47,A,B 62
ESSEX ST   FLEET ST   TOWNSEND ST
150
46A,B 86   PEARSE ST

TARA ST STATION

83
155
DAME ST
15,
15A,
15B

PEARSE STATION

CHRIST CH PL
NASSAU ST   LEINSTER ST   CLARE ST

LEGEND

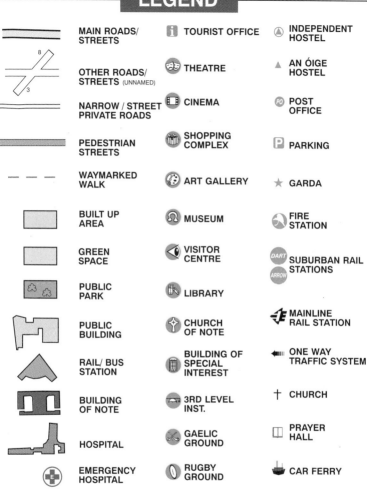

MAIN ROADS/ STREETS	**i** TOURIST OFFICE	⒜ INDEPENDENT HOSTEL
OTHER ROADS/ STREETS (UNNAMED)	🎭 THEATRE	▲ AN ÓIGE HOSTEL
NARROW / STREET PRIVATE ROADS	🎬 CINEMA	PO POST OFFICE
PEDESTRIAN STREETS	🛍 SHOPPING COMPLEX	P PARKING
– – – WAYMARKED WALK	🕐 ART GALLERY	★ GARDA
BUILT UP AREA	Ω MUSEUM	🔥 FIRE STATION
GREEN SPACE	◉ VISITOR CENTRE	DART ARROW SUBURBAN RAIL STATIONS
PUBLIC PARK	📚 LIBRARY	🚅 MAINLINE RAIL STATION
PUBLIC BUILDING	✝ CHURCH OF NOTE	◀ ONE WAY TRAFFIC SYSTEM
RAIL/ BUS STATION	🏛 BUILDING OF SPECIAL INTEREST	† CHURCH
BUILDING OF NOTE	🚗 3RD LEVEL INST.	🏛 PRAYER HALL
HOSPITAL	⚔ GAELIC GROUND	⛵ CAR FERRY
⊕ EMERGENCY HOSPITAL	🏉 RUGBY GROUND	✈ AIRPORT
WATER	⚽ SOCCER GROUND	

CALE 1:10 000
cm = 100 metres)

100m 50m 0 metres   100m   200m   300m   400m   500 metres

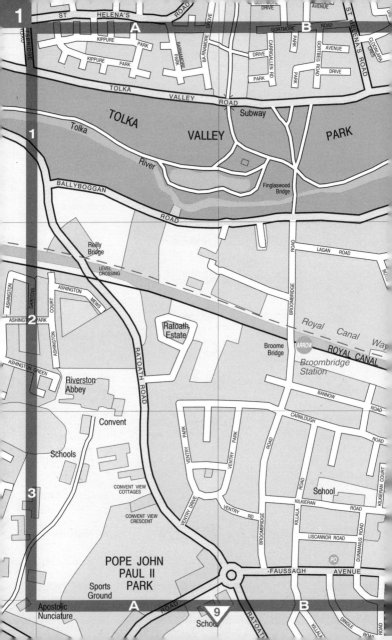

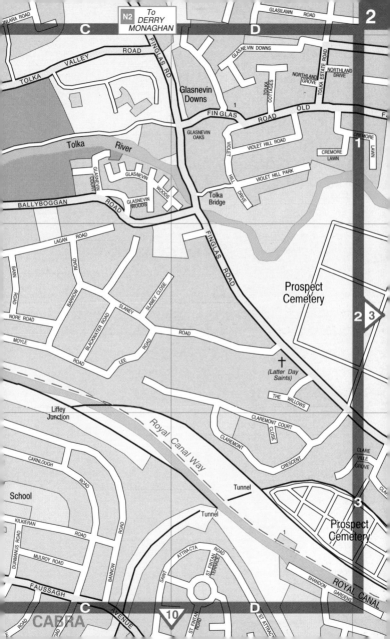

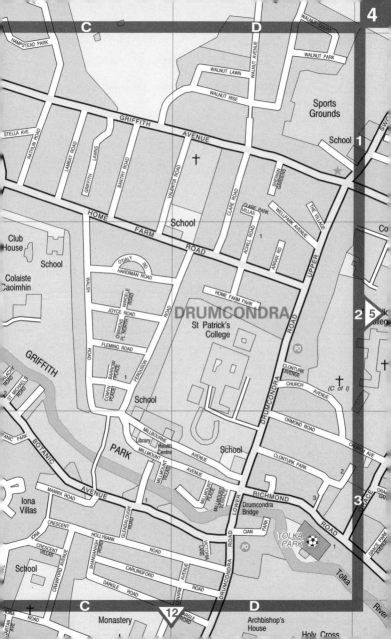

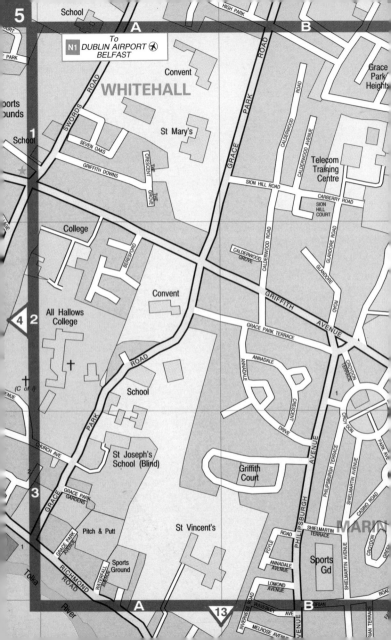

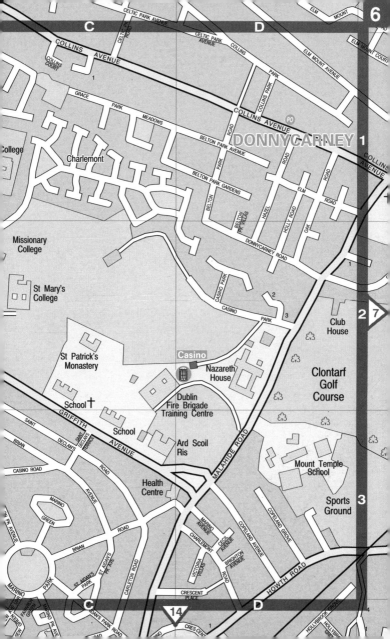

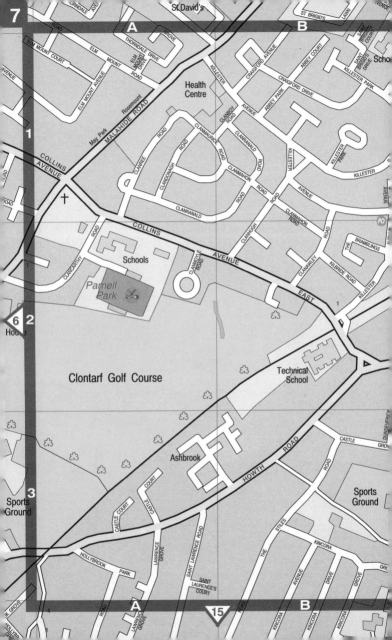

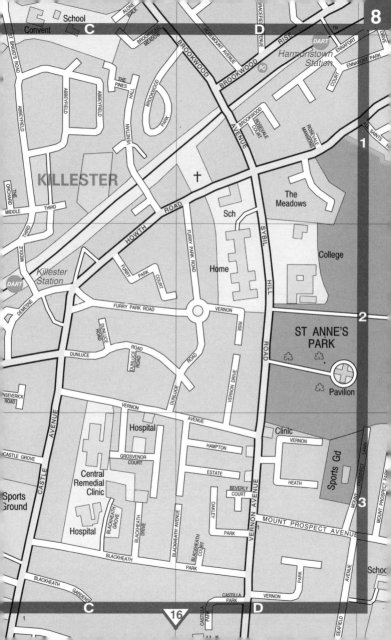

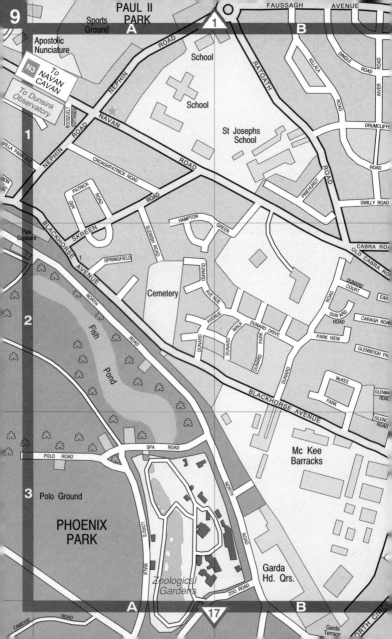

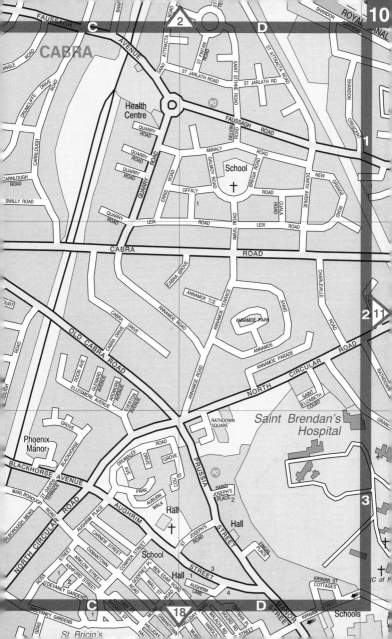

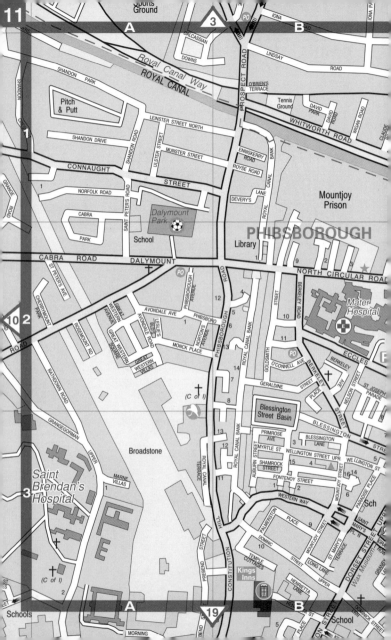

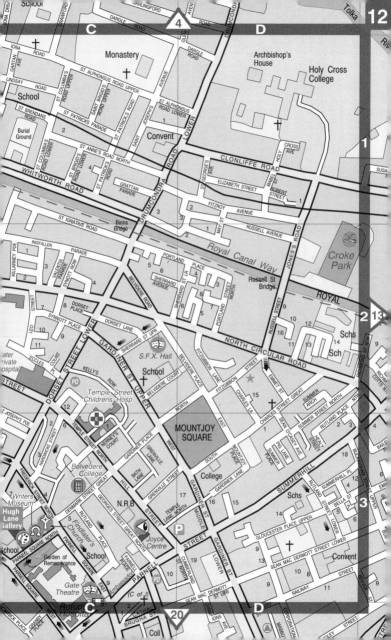

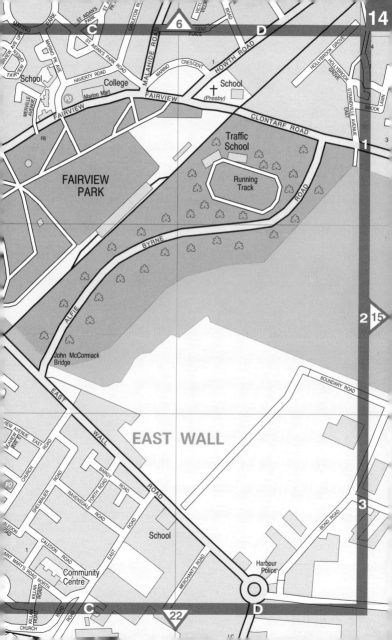

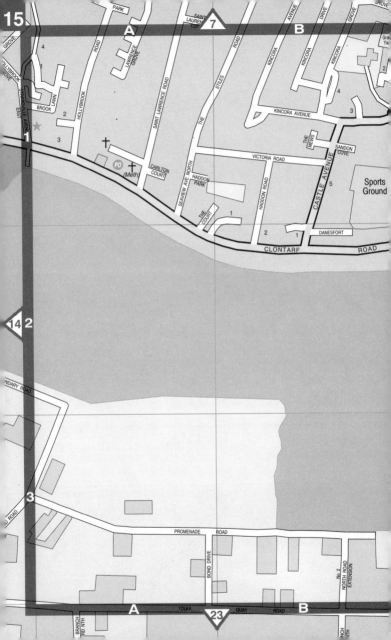

BLACKHEATH

8

VERNON

CASTILLA
PARK

CASTILLA
PARK

1

CASTLE AVENUE

SEAFIELD

Hall

SEAFIELD ROAD EAST

SEAFIELD

ROAD WEST

VERNON COURT

Schools

MERCHAMP

CASTLE ROAD

KINCORA

ROAD

CHELSEA GARDENS

1

VERNON AVENUE

KINCORA

KINCORA ROAD

OULTON ROAD

Sports
Ground

KINCORA PARK

BELGROVE ROAD

VERNON GROVE

VERNON GARDENS

Summerville

School 2

1

CLONTARF
PARK

BRIAN BORU ST.

BRIAN BORU AVENUE

CONQUER HILL

Clontarf
Baths

PO

CLONTARF PARK

CONQUER HILL
AVENUE

CLONTARF

Toilets

CLONTARF

VERNON COURT

FORTVIEW AVENUE

ROAD

2

Yacht Club
Slipway

3

TOLKA QUAY ROAD

24

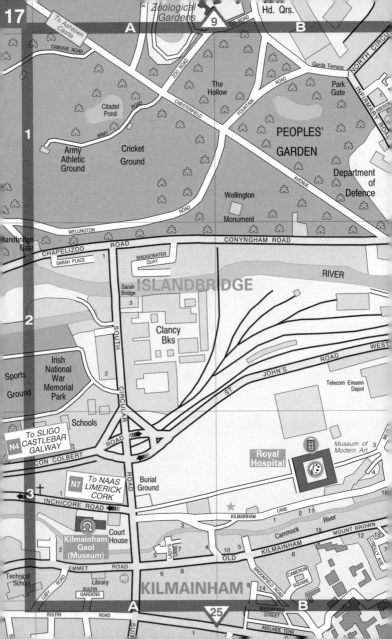

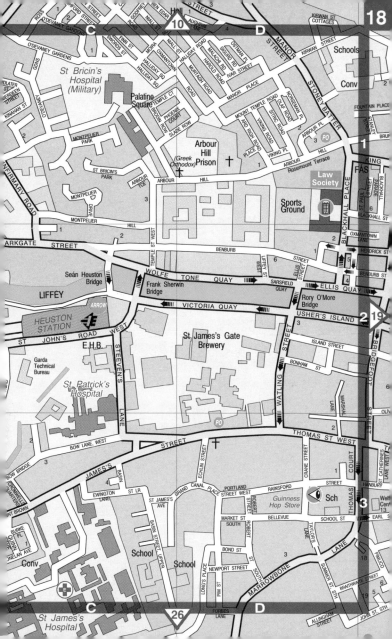

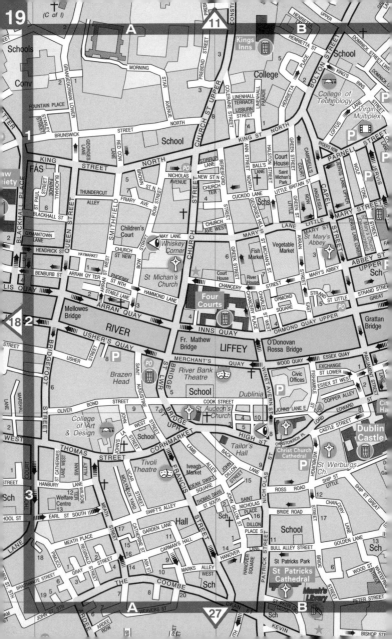

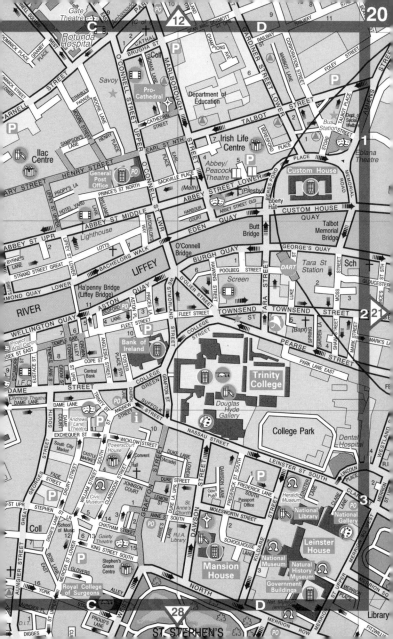

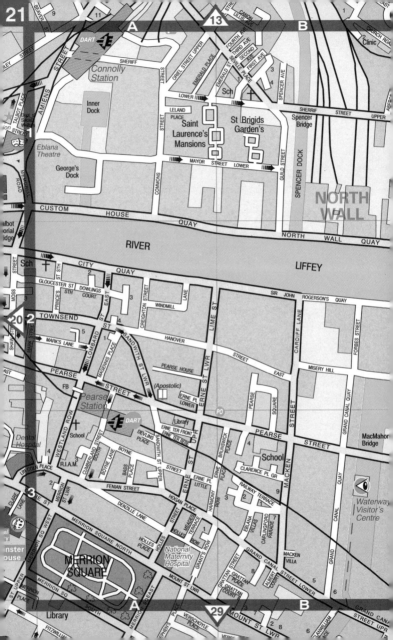

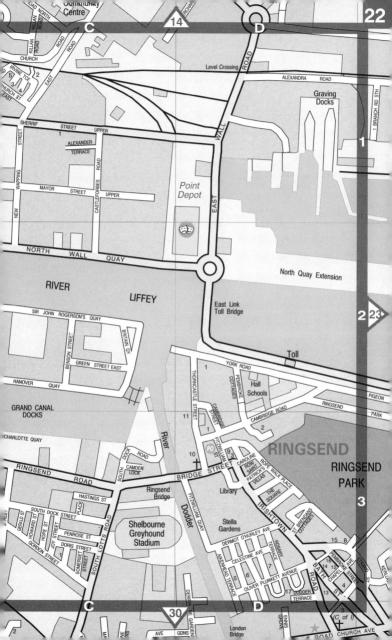

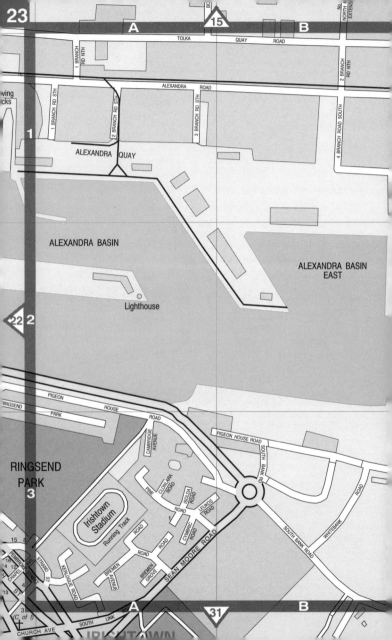

A
15
B

TOLKA QUAY ROAD

1 BRANCH RD NTH

2 BRANCH RD NTH

No.
NORTH
EXTENS

ALEXANDRA ROAD

1 BRANCH RD STH

2 BRANCH RD STH

3 BRANCH RD STH

4 BRANCH ROAD SOUTH

ving
cks

1

ALEXANDRA QUAY

ALEXANDRA BASIN

ALEXANDRA BASIN
EAST

Lighthouse

2 2

PIGEON HOUSE ROAD

RINGSEND PARK

PIGEON HOUSE ROAD

CAMBRIDGE AVENUE

SOUTH BANK RD

RINGSEND
PARK
3

Irishtown
Stadium

Running Track

PINE ROAD

CLONLARA ROAD

ISOLDA ROAD

LEUKOS ROAD

CYMRIC ROAD

ROAD

ROAD

ROAD

WHITEBANK ROAD

ROAD

SOUTH BANK ROAD

SEAN MOORE ROAD

15 8

KERLOGUE ROAD

STRAND ST

BREMEN ROAD

BREMEN GROVE

BREMEN AVENUE

PEMBROKE STREET

CHAPEL
ST

13

(C of I)

3

A
31
B

CHURCH AVE

SOUTH LINK ROAD

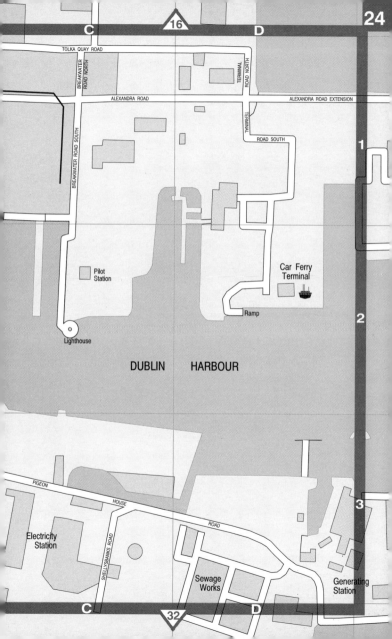

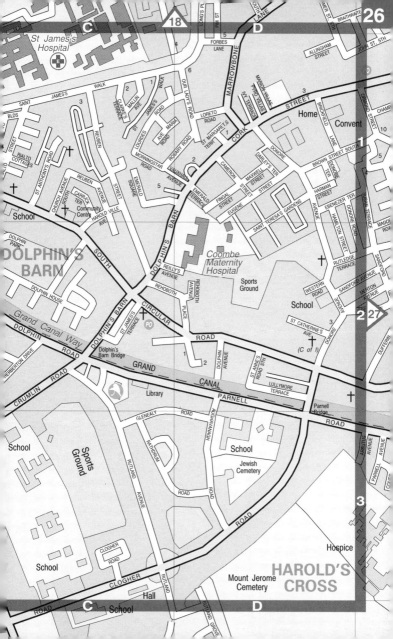

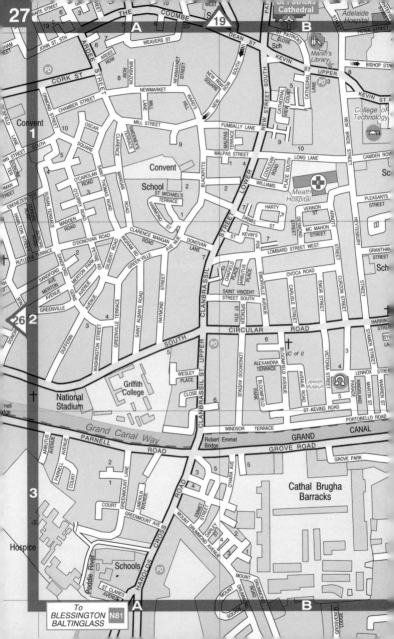

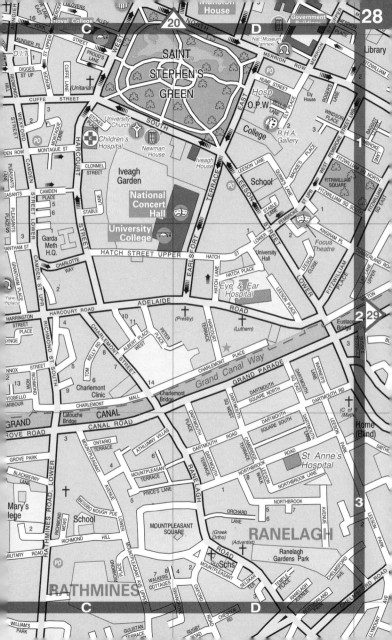

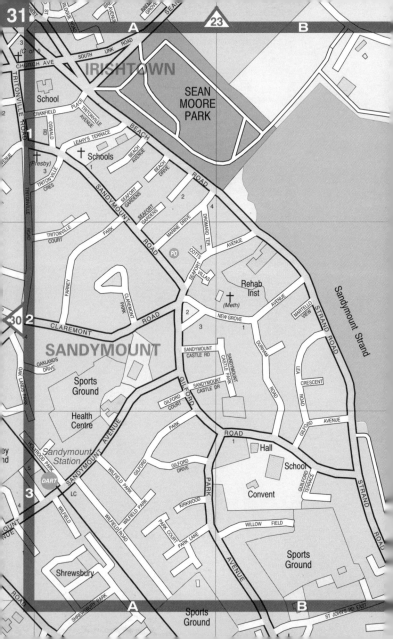

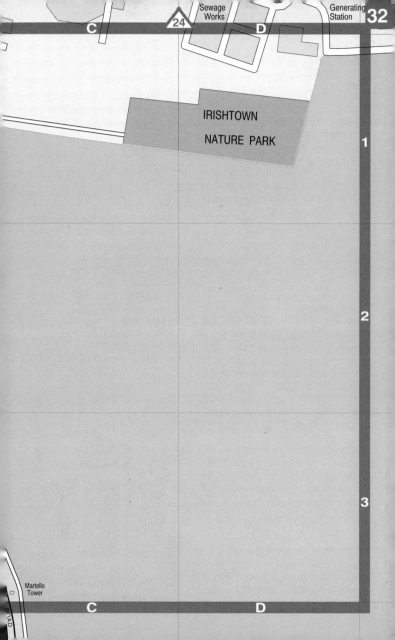

Sewage
Works

Generating
Station

IRISHTOWN

NATURE PARK

Martello
Tower

ROAD

TOURIST INFORMATION

Buildings of Note

Bank of Ireland (Former Parliament House)
College Green
Designed by Sir Edward Lovett Pearce and built between 1729 and 1739. Enlarged by James Gandon and Robert Parke between 1785 and 1794. The Bank of Ireland took over this building in 1804. It had been the scene of many dramatic events in Irish politics up to the passing of the Act of Union in 1800.
Visiting Times:
Mon/Tues/Wed/Fri
10a.m. - 4p.m.
Thurs 10a.m. - 5p.m.   20 **C2**

Belvedere House/Belvedere College,
Great Dominick Street.
Built in 1775 for George, Rochford Lord Belvedere. It was bought in 1841 by the Jesuits for use as a boys college. The building contains some fine plasterwork by Michael Stapleton and fireplaces by the Venetian Bossi.
                                        12 **C3**

Bluecoat School,
Blackhall Place.
Designed by Thomas Ivory and built in the palladian style between 1773 and 1783. The interior has some fine plasterwork by Charles Thorp. The cupola was added in 1904. It is now the home of the Incorporated Law Society.   18 **D1**

Brazen Head.
Lower Bridge Street
This is Dublin's oldest hostelery built in 1666. Its foundations which are at a lower level than the surrounding area suggest that it was built on a much older site probably Viking. It was frequented by many Irish patriots including Wolfe Tone, Robert Emmet and Daniel O'Connell.
                                        19 **A2**

Casino Marino
Malahide Road
Located 4kms from the city centre off the Malahide Road. The Casino was built in 1758 for Lord Charlemont from a design by Sir William Chambers. It has been described as one of the finest 18th century classical buildings in Ireland. Access is by guided tour only.
Visiting Times:
Feb - Mid June
12 noon - 4p.m. Sun & Wed
Mid June - Sept
9.30a.m. - 6.30p.m. Daily
Oct 10a.m. - 5p.m. Daily
Nov 12 noon - 4p.m. Sun & Wed   6 **D2**

Casino Marino

City Hall
Lord Edward Street

Formerly the Royal Exchange, designed by Thomas Cooley and completed between 1769 and 1779.

This is the headquarters for Dublin's Municipal Government. Archives dating back to the 12th Century are stored in the Muniment Room. It also houses the mace and sword of the city along with 102 Royal Charters.

Visiting Times:
Mon - Fri 9a.m. - 1p.m.
       2.15p.m. - 5p.m.   **19 B2**

The Royal College of Surgeons,
St. Stephen's Green West.

Designed by William Murray and built between 1825 to 1827. It was occupied by the Irish Citizen Army during the 1916 Rising under the command of Countess Markievicz.   **20 C3**

The Custom House
Custom House Quay

Designed by James Gandon and built between 1781 and 1791. The building was gutted by fire during the War of Independence. It was restored by the Office of Public Works after the Irish Free State was established.   **20 D1**

Dublin Castle

Built at the behest of King John in 1204 on a site which was once a Viking stronghold. It has served as a military fortress, prison, courts of law and the core of British Administration in Ireland until 1922. The Castle is now used for State functions. Guided tours of the State Apartments, Chapel Royal and Undercroft.

Visiting Times:
Mon - Fri 10a.m. - 5p.m.
Sat/Sun/Public Holidays 2 - 5p.m.   **19 B3**

General Post Office
O'Connell Street

Designed by Francis Johnston and built between 1814 and 1818.

The GPO became the focal point of the 1916 Insurrection and the Proclamation of the Irish Republic took place there. Destroyed by fire, it was restored in 1929. In the public office is a noteworthy statue representing the Death of Cuchulainn, the work of Oliver Sheppard R.H.A.   **20 C1**

The Four Courts
Inns Quay

Built between 1785 and 1802 this is one of designer James Gandons' masterpieces.

It houses the Irish Law Courts and Law Library. Destroyed by fire in 1922 it was completely restored by 1932.   **19 B2**

Dublin Castle

Government Buildings,
Upper Merrion Street.
This building was designed as the Royal College of Science by Sir Aston Webb. It was opened by King George V on his visit in 1911. Among other department offices here is the Taoiseach's office.   **20 D3**

Iveagh House,
St. Stephen's Green.
This building built in 1736 was presented to the Irish Nation in 1939 by the 2nd Earl Iveagh. It is now occupied by the Department of Foreign Affairs.   **28 D1**

Kilmainham Gaol
Inchicore Road
One of the largest decommissioned jails in Europe, it played its part in some of the most patriotic and tragic episodes that light the path of Ireland's journey to modern nationhood, from the 1780's to 1924. Featuring many exhibitions and a multi-lingual audio-visual show. Access by guided tour only.
Visiting Times:
Jan - Mid April
1p.m. - 4p.m. Mon - Fri
1p.m. - 6p.m. Sunday
Late April - Sept
9.30a.m. - 6p.m. Daily
Oct - Dec.
9.30a.m. - 5p.m. Mon - Fri
10a.m. - 6p.m. Sunday
Closed Saturday   **17 A3**

Kings Inns,
Constitution Hill.
Designed partly by James Gandon and built between 1795 and 1817. The library contains 100,000 volumes including most of the Dublin directories published and a fine collection of English county histories.
Not open to the public.   **11 B3**

Leinster House
Kildare Street
Designed by Richard Cassells this fine Georgian town house was built for the Duke of Leinster. The Royal Dublin Society occupied it until 1922 when it purchased by the Irish Free State. Since 1922 it has served as a Parliament House which is the meeting place of the Dail {Chamber of Deputies} and Seanad (Senate).   **20 D3**

The Mansion House
Dawson Street
This Queen Anne style house designed by Joshua Dawson was built in 1710. The round room was added in 1821. It has been the official residence of Dublin's Lord Mayors since 1715. The Anglo-Irish truce was signed here in 1921.   **20 D3**

Newman House,
85 - 86 St. Stephen's Green.
The Catholic University (now U.C.D.) founded here by Cardinal Newman. The poet Gerard Manley Hopkins was professor of Greek here while James Joyce and Flann O'Brien studied here. These two fine 18th century houses have been restored and are open to the public.
28 C1

Georgian Door

``Number 29'',
Lower Fitzwilliam Street.
Situated on the corner of Mount Street and Fitzwilliam Street. This typical middle-class home of the period 1790 -1820 is faithfully restored and furnished.   29 **A1**

Powerscourt House,
South William Street.
Designed by Robert Mack for Viscount Powerscourt and built between 1771 and 1774. It is now a shopping mall with shops including cafes, restaurants, crafts and antiques.   20 **C3**

The Rotunda Hospital,
Parnell Square.
The Rotunda Hospital was the first purpose built maternity hospital in the British Isles. Designed by Richard Bassels it was opened in 1757. A feature of the building is its chapel with its fine baroque plasterwork by Bartholomew Cranmillion.   20 **C1**

Royal Hospital and Irish Museum of Modern Art
Military Road, Kilmainham.
The most important 17th century building in Ireland has been restored. Guided tours available of the Master's Quarters, the Great Hall with the portrait collection, and the chapel which contains outstanding woodcarving by Tabary and a magnificent Baroque ceiling. The Irish Museum of Modern Art was established in 1991 and exhibits Irish and International art of the 20th century.
Visiting Times:
Tues - Sat 10.00a.m. - 5.30p.m.
Sun 12 noon - 5.30p.m.
Closed Monday   17 **B3**

The Shaw Birthplace,
Synge Street.
Situated at No. 33 Synge Street this is the birthplace of George Bernard Shaw the Nobel prizewinning author and playwright. Built in 1838 it also gives an insight into the life of a Victorian family.   28 **C2**

Tailors' Hall,
High Street.
Built in 1706 - 1707 this is Dublins only surviving guildhall. Restored in recent times, it now houses An Taisce the Irish National Trust.
    19 **B3**

Trinity College
College Green
Trinity is a one college university founded by Queen Elizabeth in 1592. The oldest buildings now surviving date from 1700. The multi-media presentation "The Dublin Experience" is on show 7 days a week from May to early October. See also Trinity College Library.   20 **D2**

Fountain - College Green

Parks and Gardens

Garden of Remembrance,
Parnell Square East, Dublin 1.
The Garden of Remembrance was designed by Daithí Hanly and is dedicated to the memory of those who died in the cause of Irish freedom. The garden is open daily during daylight hours.   12 **C3**

Herbert Park,
Ballsbridge.
A charming mature park, well laid out with interesting trees, shrubs and flower beds. An attractive feature is the large pond on the eastern side of the park.   30 **C3**

Irish National War Memorial Park,
Islandbridge.
Designed by the English architect Sir Edward Lutyens, these gardens are dedicated to the memory of 49,400 Irish soldiers who died in the First World War. The Gardens are open every day all year round during daylight hours.   17 **A2**

Merrion Square Park,
Merrion Square.
Formerly only for the use of the residents of Merrion Square, this public park is surrounded on all sides by some of Dublin's finest Georgian architecture.21 **A3**

National Botanic Gardens,
Botanic Road, Glasnevin.
Covering 19.5 hectares, these beautiful gardens contain a huge assortment of trees, plants and shrubs. Rare blooms and palms are housed in the huge Victorian conservatories.
Visiting Times:
Mon - Sat
9.00am - 6.00pm in summer
10.00am - 4.30pm in winter
Sundays:
11.00am - 6.00pm in summer

11.00am - 4.30pm in winter
Greenhouses not open before 2pm on Sundays. Admission free.   3 **A2**

Phoenix Park,
North-western edge of city.
Acknowledged as one of the largest enclosed urban parks in the world, it covers 1,760 acres, with a circumference of seven miles. Close to the main entrance at Parkgate Street are the People's Gardens and the Zoological Gardens (see separate entry). Within the park are the residence of the President of Ireland (Aras and Uachtarain), the American Ambassador's residence and the Ordnance Survey Office.
Visiting Times:
Phoenix Park is open to the public at all times but the People's Gardens have their own opening times, these are Monday to Saturday 10.30a.m; Sunday 10.00a.m. Closing times range between 4.00p.m. in December and January and 9.30p.m. in June and July. Parkgate entrance. 17 **B1**

Irish National War Memorial Park,

St. Anne's Park and Gardens,
Mount Prospect Avenue, Clontarf.

In a pleasant setting adjacent to Dollymount Strand, the rose gardens in this park cover over three acres alone. The Park and Gardens are open all year round. Admission free. Entrance Howth Road/All Saints Road. 8 **D2**

St. Stephen's Green.

Covering twenty-two acres at the top of Grafton Street, St. Stephen's Green is right in the heart of the city. The varied landscaping of this delightful park includes trees, flower beds, a waterfall and an artificial lake. Several notable monuments and sculptures may also be seen.

Visiting Hours:
During daylight hours from 8.00a.m. to 9.00p.m. Monday to Saturday and from 11.00a.m. on Sunday. 28 **C1**

Zoological Gardens,
Phoenix Park.

In these outstanding attractive gardens may be seen a large collection of wild animals and birds from all over the world. Spacious houses and outdoor enclosures add to the total effect. Lion breeding has a long and distinguished history at Dublin Zoo. Two natural lakes house pelicans, flamingoes, ducks and geese.

Visiting Times:
Weekdays: 9.30a.m. - 6.00p.m.
Sundays 10.30a.m. - 6.00p.m.
Gardens close at sunset in winter. 9 **A3**

The Peoples Gardens - Phoenix Park

Art Galleries

Hugh Lane Municipal Gallery of Modern Art,
Charlemont House, Parnell Square.

The building built between 1762 and 1765 was formerly the residence of Lord Charlemont. The gallery has an interesting collection of works by 19th and 20th century artists. Sir Hugh Lane who was drowned in the sinking of the Lusitania in 1915 contributed the nucleus of this collection of pictures.

Visiting Times:
Tues - Fri 9.30a.m. - 6.00p.m.
Sat 9.30a.m. - 5.00p.m.
Sun 11.00a.m. - 5.00p.m.
Closed Monday
Admission Free 12 **C3**

National Gallery,
Merrion Lawn, Merrion Square West.

The gallery which contains over 2000 pictures, consisted of only 100 pictures when it was officially opened in 1864. As well as representing all the European schools, there is a comprehensive collection of works by Irish artists. The Art Reference Library is open from Monday to Friday. There are also free public lectures and conducted hours.

Visiting Times:
Mon to Sat 10.00a.m. - 5.30p.m.
Sunday 2.00p.m. - 5.00p.m.
Thursday open till 8.30p.m.
Closed 25/26 Dec and Good Friday
Restaurant open during gallery hours.
The library is due to re-open in mid 1996 after re-furbishment. 20 **D3**

Museums

Dublin Civic Museum,
South William Street.
Occupying the former City Assembly House. It contains a permanent collection of exhibits of antiquarian and historical interest pertaining to Dublin City.
Visiting Times:
Tues - Sat 10.00a.m. - 5.30p.m.
Sunday 11.00a.m. - 2.00p.m.
Closed Monday
Admission Free   20 **C3**

Genealogical Office and Heraldic Museum,
2 Kildare Street, Dublin 2.
Visit the oldest office of state in Ireland - founded 1552. See the unique heraldic museum with its colourful display of coats of arms, banners and facility.
Avail of the Consultancy Service on ancestry tracing designed to enable you to undertake on your own the task of uncovering your Irish roots.
Visiting Hours:
Mon - Fri 10.00a.m. - 12.30p.m.
         2.00p.m. - 4.30p.m.   20 **D3**

Genealogical Office

Irish Jewish Museum,
Walworth Road.
Opened in 1985 by President Herzog of Israel who was educated in Dublin.
Housed in a restored synagogue with documents photographs and memorabilia showing the history of Irish Jews dating back over 150 years.
Visiting Times:
April to Sept
Tues/Thurs/Sun 11.00am - 3.30pm

Oct to April
Sunday Only   10.30am - 2.30pm   27 **B2**

National Museum,
Kildare Street.
The museum houses one of the most impressive collection of antiquities in Europe. Items displayed cover every age from the Stone Age to medieval times. Items of particular interest are the Tara Brooch, the Cross of Cong and the Ardagh Chalice. One of its most recent additions was the Derrynaflan Hoard which was found in a bog in Tipperary in 1980.
The main entrance is from Kildare Street but part of the natural history division is approached from Merrion Street.
Visiting Times:
Tues - Sat 10.00a.m. - 5.00p.m.
Sunday 2.00pm. - 5.00p.m.
Closed Mondays   20 **D3**

National Wax Museum,
Granby Row.
On display are life-size figures of prominent Irish historical, political, theatrical literary and sporting personalities. Taped narrations on each scene, guide one along.
Visiting Times:
Mon - Sat 10.00am - 5.30pm
Sunday 12noon - 5.30pm   11 **B3**

The Writer's Museum,
18/19 Parnell Square North.
Opened in 1991 in two restored Georgian houses. It features a display of paintings, photographs, manuscripts and other memorabilia relating to Irish writers such as Shaw, Yeats, Beckett, Wilde, O'Casey, Joyce, Behan and Swift.
Visiting Times:
Mon - Sat 10.00a.m. - 5.00p.m.
Sundays and Bank Holidays
11.30a.m. - 6.00p.m.   12 **C3**

Ashtown Castle Visitor Centre
Phoenix Park

Located 5kms from the City Centre. The Tower House close to the visitor centre possibly dates from the 17th Century. There are exhibitions, a film show and visitors can view a colourful and realistic interpretation of the past.

Visiting Times:
Nov - Mid March
9.30a.m. - 4.30p.m. Sat/Sun
Mid March - Late March
9.30a.m. - 5.00p.m. Daily
April/May
9.30a.m. - 5.30p.m.
June/Sept
9.30a.m. - 6.30p.m.
Oct 9.30a.m. - 5.00p.m.
Last admission 45 minutes before closing.
9 **A3**

Dublinia - Christ Church
St. Michael's Hill

The realistic and novel exhibition that is Dublinia is situated in the old Synod Hall on St. Michael's Hill, alongside of Christ Church Cathedral, to which it is connected by an ornate pedestrian archway over St. Michael's Hill.

The exhibition heralds the arrival of the Anglo-Normans in 1170 through a broad spectrum of Dublin life to the closure of the Monasteries in 1540.

Visiting Times:
Summer
10a.m. - 5p.m. every day
Winter (Oct 1st - March 31st)
Mon - Sat 11a.m. - 4p.m.
Sun 10a.m. - 4.30p.m.
19 **B3**

Dunsink Observatory
Dunsink Lane, near Castleknock

Founded in 1783, this is one of the world's oldest observatories. It formerly belonged to Trinity College but is now the centre of the School of Astronomical Physics of the Dublin Institute for Advanced Studies.

Visiting Times:
Open to the public on the first and third Wednesday of each month from September to March, between 8p.m. and 10p.m. Admission free on written application to the secretary enclosing stamp-addressed envelope.
9 **A1**

The James Joyce Centre,
35 North Great Georges Street.

The centre is housed in a beautifully restored 18th century Georgian Townhouse only 300 metres from O'Connell Street. The aim of the centre is to promote an interest in the life and works of James Joyce and to this end there are daily talks, conducted tours of the house and walks through the heartland of Joyce's North inner city.
12 **C3**

Waterways Visitor Centre
Grand Canal Quay, Dublin 2.

The centre houses an exhibition outlining the history of Ireland's Inland Waterways and the activities and experiences currently available.

Featuring an audio-visual show and working models of various engineering features.

Visiting Times:
June - September
9.30a.m. - 6.30p.m. daily
Oct - May
12.30p.m. - 5p.m. Wed and Sun
Last admission 45 minutes before closing.
21 **B3**

Waterways Visitor Centre

Churches and Cathedrals

Christ Church Cathedral
Christchurch Place

Built in 1173 by Strongbow on a site originally occupied by a church built in 1030 by Sitric the Viking King. The present structure dates from the 19th century, although the medieval crypt still remains. It contains many interesting historical remains.

Visiting Times:
May - Sept (Incl) 10a.m. - 5p.m.
Oct - April (Incl) 9.30a.m. - 5p.m.
Group tours available on request/ application.   19 **B3**

St. Anne's Church,
Dawson Street.

Designed by Isaac Wells in neoromamesque style in 1720. The facade was added by Sir Thomas Deane in 1868.
                                                    20 **D3**

St. Audoen's Church
High Street

St. Audoen's dates from medieval times and is the oldest of Dublin's parish churches. The tower houses Ireland's three most ancient bells, dating from 1423. St. Audoen's Arch stands nearby. This is Dublin's only surviving city gate.

Visiting Times:
May - Sept (incl)
2.30p.m. - 5p.m. Sat/Sun
Group tours available on request phone 4542274.   19 **A3**

St. Mary's Abbey
Meetinghouse Lane (off Capel St.)

The Abbey was founded in 1139 as a daughter house of the Benedictine Order of Savigny. It was one of the largest and most important monasteries in Ireland. The Chapter House is all that remains of the Abbey which houses an interesting historical exhibition.

Visiting Times:
Mid June - Mid Sept.
10.00a.m. - 5p.m. Wed. only.   19 **B2**

St. Mary's Church
Mary Street

Dating from 1627, this was the first Dublin church to be built with galleries. Theobald Wolfe Tone was baptised here in 1763 and Sean O'Casey the playwright in 1880. This church is now a retail outlet.   19 **B1**

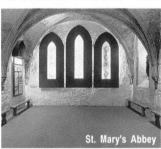

St. Mary's Abbey

St. Mary's Pro Cathedral
Marlborough Street

Designed by John Sweetman and built between 1815 and 1825 in the Great Down Style. The Metropolitan Church of the diocese, it is used for state functions.
                                                    20 **C1**

St. Michan's Church
Church Street

Founded by the Norse in 1096, the present building dates from 1685-6, having been much restored in 1828. The church's Harris organ is said to have been used by Handel during his visit to Dublin. Vaults beneath the church contain mummified corpses which may be seen by the public.

Visiting Times:
Church and Vaults:
April - Oct
10a.m. - 5p.m. Mon - Fri
Nov - March
12.30p.m. - 3.30p.m. Mon - Fri
10a.m. - 1p.m. Saturday
Vaults closed on Sunday   19 **A2**

St. Patrick's Cathedral, Patrick Street.

Built on the site of a 6th century church said to have been founded by St.Patrick himself. The present church was commenced in 1191. In 1213 it gained Cathedral status. A university was established there in 1320 but was suppressed by Henry VIII. The square tower was build in the 14th century and houses the largest ringing bells in Ireland. Jonathan Swift was Dean of St. Patricks from 1713 to 1745.

Visiting Times:
Mon - Fri 9a.m. - 6p.m.
Saturday 9a.m. - 5p.m.
Sunday 10a.m. - 4.30p.m.
Closed 4p.m. Nov - March   19 **B3**

St. Werburgh's Church Werburgh Street

Erected in 1715 on the site of the medieval successor to pre Norman St. Werburgh's. Destroyed by fire in 1754, the church was re-opened in 1759. In the vaults beneath the church is buried Lord Edward Fitzgerald.

Visiting Times:
By appointment only
Tel: (01) 4783710
Mon - Fri 10.00a.m. - 4.00p.m.   19 **B3**

University Church, St. Stephens Green.

Founded by Cardinal Newman, it was designed in a neo-Byzantine style by John Hungerford Pollen. It was built between 1854 and 1856.

28 **C1**

St. Patrick's Cathedral

Libraries

Chester Beatty Library,
20 Shrewsbury Road.
One of the world's most valuable private collections of oriental manuscripts and miniatures can be seen here. There are manuscripts of the New Testament, Manichean papyri and Eastern miniatures, as well as picture scrolls, albums and jades from the Far East.
Visiting Times:
Tues - Fri 10.00a.m. - 5.00p.m.
Saturday 2p.m. - 5p.m.
Closed Mondays
Closed Tues following Bank Holidays
Guided Tours Wed/Sat From 2.30p.m.
Admission Free.   30 **D3**

Marsh's Library,
St. Patrick's Close.
This is Ireland's oldest public library, founded in 1701 by Archbishop Narcissus Marsh. The collection consists mainly of theological, medical, ancient historical, Hebrew, Syriac, Greek, French and Latin literature.
Visiting Hours:
Weekdays 10.00a.m. - 12.45p.m.
            2.00p.m. - 5.00p.m.
Sat 10.30a.m. - 12.45p.m.
Closed Tuesdays, Sundays and Bank Holidays.   27 **B1**

National Library,
Kildare Street.
Founded in 1877 this is Ireland's largest public library. It contains over half a million books as well as maps, prints and manuscripts. It also houses a large newspaper collection.
Visiting Times:
Mon 10.00a.m. - 9.00p.m.
Tues/Wed 2.00p.m. - 9.00p.m.
Thurs/Fri 10.00a.m. - 5.00p.m.
Saturday 10.00a.m. to 1.00p.m.   20 **D3**

Royal Irish Academy Library,
19 Dawson Street.
One of the most extensive collections of ancient Irish manuscripts can be seen here. These include the "Book of the Dun Cow" the "Book of Ballymote", the "Speckled Book" the "Slowe Missal" and the Cathac or Battle Book reputed to be the actual copy of the Psalms made in the 6th century by St. Colmcille.
Visiting Times:
Mon - Fri 10.30a.m. - 5.15p.m.
Closed Bank Holidays and during the last three weeks of August.
Admission Free.   20 **D3**

Trinity College - Entrance

Trinity College Library,
College Green.
Dating from the late sixteenth century, Trinity College Library is Ireland's oldest library. It contains over 1,000,000 volumes and Ireland's most extensive collection of manuscripts and early printed books. Its greatest treasure is the Book of Kells (probably eighth century).
The library is housed in two buildings - the Old Library (completed in 1732) and the New Library (1967).
Visiting Times
Mon - Sat 9.30a.m. to 5.p.m.
October - May
Sun 12.00noon to 4.30p.m.
June - September
Sun 9.30a.m. to 5.00p.m.   20 **D2**

Street name	Page/Grid Ref.
1 Branch Rd N	23 A1
1 Branch Rd S	23 A1
2 Branch Rd N	23 B1
2 Branch Rd S	23 A1
3 Branch Rd S	23 A1
4 Branch Rd S	23 B1
Abbey Cottages	20 C2[2]
Abbey Court	7 B1
Abbey Park	7 B1
Abbey Street Lr	20 D1
Abbey Street Mid	20 C2
Abbey Street Old	20 D1
Abbey Street Upr	19 B2
Abbeyfield	8 C1
Abercorn Road	21 B1
Aberdeen Street	18 C1
Achill Road	4 D2
Adair	30 D3[4]
Adair Lane	20 C2[3]
Addison Place	3 B2
Addison Road	13 B1
Adelaide Road	28 C2
Adelaide Terrace	25 B1
Aikenhead Terrace	22 D3
Albert Court	21 B3
Albert Place East	21 B3[8]
Albert Place West	28 C2
Albert Terrace	28 C2[11]
Aldborough Parade	13 A3
Aldborough Place	13 A3
Aldborough Square	13 A3[12]
Alexandra Road	23 A1
Alexandra Rd Ext	24 D1
Alexander Terrace (North Wall)	22 C1
Alexandra Terrace	27 B2
Alexandra Quay	23 A1
Alfie Byrne Road	14 C2
Allingham Street	26 D1
Almeida Avenue	17 B3[8]
Almeida Terrace	25 B1[1]
Alverno	15 B2[1]
Amiens Street	13 A3
Anglesea Road	30 C3
Anglesea Row	19 B1
Angelesea Street	20 C2
Annadale Avenue	5 B3
Annadale Crescent	5 B2
Annadale Drive	5 B2
Annaly Road	10 D1
Annamoe Drive	10 D2
Annamoe Parade	10 D2
Annamoe Park	10 D2
Annamoe Road	10 C2
Annamoe Terrace	10 D2
Anne Street North	19 B1
Anne Street South	20 C3
Anne's Lane	20 C3
Anner Road	25 A1
Annesley Avenue	13 B2[2]
Annesley Bridge Rd	13 B2
Annesley Place	13 B2
Aranmore Avenue	11 B2[9]
Arbour Hill	18 C1
Arbour Place	18 D1
Arbour Terrace	18 C1
Arbutus Avenue	27 A3
Arbutus Place	27 B2
Ard Righ Place	18 D1
Ard Righ Road	18 D1
Ardagh Road	25 B3
Ardee Grove	27 B3
Ardee Road	28 C3
Ardee Row	27 A1
Ardee Street	27 A1
Ardilaun Road	13 A2
Ardmore Avenue	10 C2
Ardoyne House	29 B3[3]
Ardpatrick Road	9 A1
Argyle Road	29 B3
Arklow Street	10 C3
Armstrong Street	27 A3[3]
Army Road	17 A1
Arnott Street	27 B1
Arran Road	4 D2
Arran Street East	19 B2
Arran Street West	19 A2
Arran Quay	19 A2
Arran Quay Terrace	19 A2
Asdill's Row	20 C2[5]
Ash Grove	19 A3[14]
Ash Street	19 A3
Ashbrook	7 A3
Ashford Cottages	10 C3[2]
Ashford Place	10 C3[1]
Ashford Street	10 C3
Ashington Court	1 A2
Ashington Mews	1 A2
Ashling Close	25 B3
Ashmount Court	17 A3[8]
Ashworth Place	27 B3[3]
Aston Place	20 C2
Aston Quay	20 C2
Athlumney Villas	28 C3
Auburn Street	11 B3
Auburn Terrace	17 B3[10]
Auburn Walk	10 C3
Aughavanagh Rd	26 D3
Aughrim Court	10 D3[4]
Aughrim Lane	10 D3
Aughrim Place	10 C3
Aughrim Street	10 C3
Aughrim Villas	10 D3[1]
Aungier Lane	28 C1[1]
Aungier Place	28 C1
Aungier Street	20 C3
Austin's Cottages	13 B2[10]
Ave Maria Road	26 C1
Avenue Road	27 B2
Avondale Avenue	11 A2
Avondale House	12 D3[19]
Avondale Road	11 A2
Bachelor's Walk	20 C2
Bachelor's Way	20 C2
Back Lane	19 B3
Baggot Court	29 A1
Baggot Street Lwr	29 A1
Baggot Street Upr	29 A2
Baggotrath Place	29 A1[2]
Bailey's Row	13 A3
Balfe Street	20 C3[3]
Ball's Lane	19 B1
Ballsbridge	30 C3
Ballsbridge Avenue	30 C3
Ballsbridge Park	30 D3[6]
Ballsbridge Terrace	30 C3[1]
Ballsbridge Wood	30 C2
Ballyboggan Road	1 A1
Ballybough Avenue	13 A2[15]
Ballybough Court	13 A2[14]
Ballybough Lane	13 A2[12]
Ballybough Road	13 A2
Ballygall Road East	3 A1
Ballymun Road	3 B1
Bangor Drive	25 B3
Bangor Road	25 B3
Bann Road	2 C2
Bannaville	28 C3[4]
Bannow Road	1 B2
Bantry Road	4 C1
Bargy Road	14 C3
Barnamore Grove	1 A1
Barnamore Park	1 A1
Barrack Lane	30 D1[3]
Barrow Place	4 C2
Barrow Road	2 C2
Barrow Street	22 C3
Basin Street Lwr	18 C3
Basin Street Upr	18 C3
Bass Place	21 A3
Bath Avenue	30 C1
Bath Ave Gdns	30 C1

Bath Avenue Place	30 C1	Blackhall Place	18 D2	Brian Boru Avenue	16 D2
Bath Lane	12 C3	Blackhall Street	19 A1	Brian Boru Street	16 D2
Bath Street	22 D3	Blackheath Avenue	8 C3	Brian Terrace	13 B1
Bayview Avenue	13 A2	Blackheath Court	8 D3	Brian Road	6 C3/13 B1
Beach Avenue	31 A1	Blackheath Drive	8 C3	Brickfield Drive	25 B2
Beach Drive	31 A1	Blackheath Gardens	8 C3	Brickfield Lane	26 D1
Beach Road	31 A1	Blackheath Grove	8 C3	Bride Road	19 B3
Beatty's Avenue	30 C2	Blackheath Park	8 C3	Bride Street	19 B3
Beaucourt	4 D2[1]	Blackhorse Avenue	9 A2	Bride Close	19 B2[17]
Beaver Close	13 A3[9]	Blackhorse Grove	10 C3	Bride Court	19 B3[17]
Beaver Street	13 A3	Blackpitts	27 A1	Bridge Court	29 B1[8]
Bective Square	11 B2[13]	Blackwater Road	2 C2	Bridge Street	22 D3
Bedford Lane	20 C2	Blessington Court	11 B3[7]	Bridge Street Lower	19 A2
Bedford Row	20 C2[4]	Blessington Lane	11 B3	Bridge Street Upper	19 A3
Belgrove Road	16 D1	Blessington Street	11 B3	Bridgefoot Street	19 A2
Bell's Lane	28 D1	Bloomfield Avenue	27 B2	Bridgewater Quay	17 A2
Bella Avenue	12 D3[7]	Bloomfield Avenue	29 A3	Brighton Avenue	6 D3
Bella Place	12 D3[6]	(Ranelagh)		Britain Place	12 C3[10]
Bella Street	12 D3	Bloomfield Cottages	27 B2[6]	Britain Quay	22 C2
Bellevue	18 D3	Bloomfield Park	27 B2	Broadstone Avenue	11 B3[12]
Bellevue Cottages	2 D1[1]	Blythe Avenue	21 B1[2]	Brodin Row	18 C1
Bellman's Walk	21 B1[4]	Boardman's Lane	26 C1[5]	Brookfield Road	17 B3
Belmont Place	12 D3[16]	Bond Drive	15 A3	Brookfield Street	25 B1
Belton Park Avenue	6 D1	Bond Road	14 D3	Brooklawn	15 A1
Belton Park Gardens	6 D1	Bond Street	18 D3	Brookwood Ave	8 D1
Belton Park Road	6 D1	Bonham Street	18 D2	Brookwood Glen	8 D1
Belton Park Villas	6 D2	Boolavogue Road	14 C3[1]	Brookwood Meadow	8 C1
Belvidere Avenue	12 D2[5]	Borris Court	19 B3[5]	Brookwood Park	8 C1
Belvidere Court	12 C2	Botanic Avenue	4 C3	Brookwood Rise	8 D1
Belvidere Place	12 D2	Botanic Road	3 B3	Broombridge Road	1 B2
Belvidere Road	12 C2	Botanic Park	4 C3	Brown Street North	19 A1
Ben Edar Road	10 C3	Botanic Villas	3 B3	Brown Street South	26 D1
Benbulbin Avenue	25 A2	Boundary Road	14 D2	Brunswick Place	21 B3
Benbulbin Rd	25 A2	Bow Bridge	18 C3	Brunswick St Nth	19 A1
Benburb Street	18 D2	Bow Lane East	20 C3	Brunswick Villas	20 D2[4]
Bengal Terrace	3 A3	Bow Lane West	18 C3	Buckingham Place	13 A3[6]
Benson Street	22 C2	Bow Street	19 A1	Buckingham St Lwr	13 A3
Beresford	5 A2	Boyne Lane	21 A3	Buckingham St Upr	13 A3
Beresford Place	20 D1	Boyne Road	1 B2	Buckingham Village	12 D3[12]
Beresford Street	19 B1	Boyne Street	21 A3	Bulfin Gardens	17 A3
Berkeley Avenue	11 B2	Brabazon Place	27 A1[8]	Bulfin Road	25 A1
Berkeley Mews	30 C1[5]	Brabazon Row	27 A1	Bull Alley Street	19 B3
Berkeley Place	11 B2	Brabazon Square	19 A3[1]	Burgess Lane	19 A2[1]
Berkeley Road	11 B2	Brabazon Street	19 A3[7]	Burgh Quay	20 D2
Berkeley Street	11 B2	Bracken's Lane	20 D2[3]	Burke Place	18 C3
Berkeley Terrace	30 C1	Brainsboro Terrace	27 A2[4]	Burleigh Court	29 A2
Berystede	29 A3[2]	Braithwaite Street	18 D3	Burlington Gardens	29 A2
Bessborough Ave	13 B2	Brandon Terrace	26 D1[4]	Burlington Road	29 A2
Bessborough Pde	28 C3	Breakwater Rd Nth	24 C1	Byrne's Lane	20 C2
Bethany House	31 B3[1]	Breakwater Rd Sth	24 C1	Cabra	10 C1
Bethesda Place	12 C3[8]	Bregia Road	10 D1	Cabra Drive	10 C2
Beverly Court	8 D3	Bremen Avenue	23 A3	Cabra Grove	10 C2
Bishop Street	27 B1	Bremen Grove	23 A3	Cabra Park	11 A1
Black Street	17 B1[2]	Bremen Road	23 A3	Cabra Road	10 C2
Blackberry Lane	28 C3	Brenden Behan Ct	12 D2[16]	Cadogan Road	13 B1
Blackhall Parade	19 A1	Brian Avenue	6 C3	Calderwood Avenue	5 B1

Calderwood Grove 5 B2
Calderwood Road 5 B1
Caledon Road 14 C3
Camac Terrace 17 B3[16]
Cambridge Avenue 23 A3
Cambridge Court 22 D3[1]
Cambridge Road 22 D3
Cambridge Street 22 D2
Cambridge Terrace 28 D3
Camden Buildings 28 C1[6]
Camden Court 28 C2[1]
Camden Lock 22 C3
Camden Market 28 C2[3]
Camden Place 28 C1
Camden Row 27 B1
Camden St Lwr 28 C1
Camden St Old 28 C2[2]
Camden St Upr 28 C2
Camden Villas 28 C1[5]
Cameron Square 17 B3
Cameron Street 26 D1
Camogie Road 17 A1
Campbell's Court 19 B1
Campbell's Lane 12 D2[6]
Campbell's Row 12 D2[7]
Canal Road 28 C3
Canon Lillis Avenue 13 B3
Canon Mooney Gdns 22 D3[2]
Caragh Court 13 B1[1]
Caragh Road 9 B2
Carberry Road 5 B1
Carbury Terrace 22 C1[1]
Cardiff Lane 21 B2
Cards Lane 20 D2[5]
Carleton Road 6 C3
Carlingford Parade 21 B3
Carlingford Road 4 C3
Carlisle Street 27 B2
Carlton Court 15 A1
Carlton Villas 30 C2[3]
Carman's Hall 19 A3
Carnew Street 10 C3
Carnlough Road 1 B3/10 C1
Caroline Row 22 D3
Carrick Terrace 26 C1
Carrickfoyle Tce 17 A3[5]
Carrigallen Drive 1 B1
Carrigallen Park 1 B1
Carrigallen Road 1 B1
Casino Park 6 D2
Casino Road 5 B3
Castilla Park 8 D3
Castle Avenue 8 C3/15 B1
Castle Court 7 A3
Castle Grove 7 B3
Castle Market 20 C3

Castle Road 16 C1
Castle Street 19 B3
Castle Terrace 11 A2[1]
Castleforbes Road 22 C1
Cathal Brugha St 20 C1
Cathedral Lane 27 B1
Cathedral Street 20 C1
Cathedral View Ct 27 B1
Cathedral View Wk 27 B1[5]
Catherine Court 13 A2[17]
Catherine Lane N 19 A1[3]
Catherine Street 19 A3
Cavendish Row 12 C3[9]
Ceannt Fort 17 B3[9]
Cecil Avenue 6 D3
Cecilia Street 20 C2[8]
Celestine Avenue 22 D3
Celtic Park Avenue 6 D1
Celtic Park Road 6 C1
Chamber Street 27 A1
Champion Quay 20 C2[11]
Champion's Avenue 20 D1
Chancery Lane 19 B3
Chancery Place 19 B2
Chancery Street 19 B2
Chapel Avenue 22 D3
Chapel Lane 19 B1
Charlemont 6 C1
Charlemont Grdns 28 C2[7]
Charlemont Mall 28 C2
Charlemont Parade 13 A2[8]
Charlemont Place 28 C2[14]
Charlemont Place 28 D2
Charlemont Road 6 D3
Charlemont Street 28 C2
Charles Lane 12 D2
Charles St Gt 12 D3
Charles St W 19 B2
Charleville Avenue 13 A2
Charleville Mall 13 A2
Charleville Road 10 D2
Charlotte Quay 22 C3
Charlotte Way 28 C2
Chatham Court 20 C3[14]
Chatham Lane 20 C3[2]
Chatham Row 20 C3[5]
Chatham Street 20 C3
Chelmsford Avenue 28 D3
Chelmsford Road 29 A3
Chelsea Gardens 16 D1
Cheltenham Place 28 C3[3]
Cherrymount Cres 6 D2[3]
Cherrymount Grove 6 D2[2]
Cherrymount Park 11 A2
Chesterfield Avenue 17 A1
Christchurch Place 19 B3

Christchurch Sq 19 B3[9]
Church Avenue 3 B1
Church Avenue 4 D2
(Drumcondra)
Church Avenue 22 C1[4]
(East Wall)
Church Avenue
(Irishtown) 30 D1
Church Ave S 26 C1
Church Ave W 19 A1
Church Lane 20 C2
Church Lane South 27 B1[6]
Church Place 22 C1[3].
Church Road 13 B3
Church Road 14 C3
Church Row 22 C1[5]
Church Street 19 A2
Church St East 22 C1
Church St New 19 A2
Church St Upr 19 A1
Church Terrace 19 A1
Churchgate Avenue 16 D2[1]
Churchill Terrace 30 D3[5]
Cian Park 4 D3
City Quay 21 A2
Clanawley Road 7 B2
Clanboy Road 7 B1
Clanbrassil Close 27 A2
Clanbrassil St Lwr 27 A2
Clanbrassil St Upr 27 A2
Clancarthy Road 7 A2
Clandonagh Road 7 A1
Clanhugh Road 7 B2
Clanmahon Road 7 B1
Clanmaurice Road 7 A1
Clanmoyle Road 7 A2
Clanranald Road 7 A1
Clanree Road 7 A1
Clanwilliam Court 29 B1[6]
Clanwilliam Place 29 B1
Clanwilliam Square 21 B3[5]
Clanwilliam Terrace 21 B3[6]
Clare Lane 20 D3
Clare Park Villas 4 D1
Clare Road 4 D1
Clare Street 20 D3
Claremont Avenue 3 B1
Claremont Close 2 D3
Claremont Court 2 D2
(Glasnevin)
Claremont Court 30 D2[4]
(Sandymount)
Claremont Crescent 2 D2
Claremont Lawns 3 A3
Claremont Park 31 A2
Claremont Road 31 A2

Clarence Mangan Rd 27 A1
Clarence Mangan Sq 19 B3[16]
Clarence Pl Gt 21 B3
Clarence St Gr N 13 A3
Clarendon Market 20 C3[6]
Clarendon Row 20 C3[13]
Clarendon Street 20 C3
Clareville Court 3 A3
Clareville Grove 3 A3
Clarke's Terrace 26 C1
Claude Road 11 B1
Cliftonville Road 3 B3
Clinch's Court 13 A2[6]
Clogher Road 26 C3
Clonard Road 25 A3
Clonlara Road 23 A3
Clonliffe Avenue 13 A2
Clonliffe Gardens 13 A1
Clonliffe Road 12 D1/13 A1
Clonmel Street 28 C1
Clonmore Court 3 B1
Clonmore Road 13 A2
Clonmore Terrace 13 A2
Clonmore Villas 13 A2[4]
Clontarf Park 16 D2
Clontarf Road 14 D1/16 D2
Clonturk Avenue 4 D2
Clonturk Gardens 4 D3[2]
Clonturk Park 4 D3
Cloonlara Crescent 1 B1
Clyde Lane 29 B3
Clyde Road 29 B3
Coburg Street 13 A3
Coke Lane 19 A2[2]
Coke Ovens Cotts 2 D3[1]
Colbert's Fort 26 C1[2]
Coleraine Street 19 B1
College Lane 21 A3[4]
College Green 20 C2
College Street 20 D2
Collins Avenue 6 C1
Collins Avenue East 7 A2
Collins Court 6 C1
Collins Park 6 D1
Commons Street 21 A1
Comyn Place 4 C2
Con Colbert Road 17 A3
Connaught Parade 11 A1[1]
Connaught Street 11 A1
Conquer Hill Ave 16 D2
Constitution Hill 11 B3
Constitution Hill (Flats) 19 B1[3]
Convent Avenue 13 A1
Convent Close 29 A1[1]
Convent Place 28 D2[1]
Convent View Cotts 1 A3

Convent View Cres 1 A3
Conway Court 21 B3[9]
Conyngham Road 17 B2
Cook Street 19 A2
Coolevin Road 27 B1
Coombe Court 19 A3[8]
Cope Street 20 C2
Copeland Avenue 6 D3
Copeland Grove 6 D3
Copper Alley 19 B2
Coppinger Row 20 C3[4]
Cork Hill 19 B2[8]
Cork Street 26 D1
Corn Exchange Pl 20 D2[1]
Cornmarket 19 A3
Corporation Street 20 D1
Countess Markievicz 21 A2[5]
  House
Courtney Place 13 B2[1]
Cow Parlour 27 A1[4]
Cowley Place Lwr 11 B2[3]
Cowley Place Upr 11 B2[2]
Cowper Street 10 C3
Craigford Avenue 7 B1
Craigford Drive 7 B1
Crampton Court 20 C2[9]
Crane Lane 19 B2
Crane Street 18 D3
Cranfield Place 31 A1
Cranmer Lane 29 B1[1]
Crawford Avenue 4 C3
Creighton Street 21 A2
Cremore Avenue 3 A1
Cremore Crescent 3 A1
Cremore Drive 3 A1
Cremore Lawn 2 D1
Cremore Park 3 A1
Cremore Road 3 A1
Crescent Gardens 13 B2
Crescent House 14 D1[1]
Crescent Place 6 D3
Crescent Villas 4 C3
Croagh Patrick Rd 9 A1
Cromwell's Quarters 18 C3
Crosbie House 28 D3[5]
Cross Kevin Street 27 B1[8]
Crostick Alley 19 A3[15]
Crow Street 20 C2
Crown Alley 20 C2
Croydon Gardens 5 B3
Croydon Green 5 B3
Croydon Pk Ave 6 C3
Croydon Terrace 5 B3
Crumlin Road 25 A3
Cuala Road 10 D1
Cuckoo Lane 19 B1

Cuffe Lane 28 C1
Cuffe Street 28 C1
Cullen's Wood 28 D3[7]
Cumberland St Nth 12 D3
Cumberland Court 21 A3[3]
Cumberland Road 29 A2
Cumberland St Sth 21 A3
Curzon Street 27 B2
Custom Ho. Quay 20 D1
Cymbric Road 23 A3
D'Olier Street 20 D2
Dalcassian Downs 11 A1
Dalymount 11 A2
Dame Court 20 C2
Dame Lane 20 C2
Dame Street 20 C2
Danesfort 15 B2
Daneswell Road 3 B3
Daniel Street 27 B1
Dargle Road 4 C3
Darley Street 27 A3
Darley's Terrace 26 D1
Dartmouth Lane 28 D3
Dartmouth Place 28 D3
Dartmouth Road 28 D3
Dartmouth Sq E 28 D3
Dartmouth Sq N 28 D2
Dartmouth Sq Sth 28 D3
Dartmouth Sq W 28 D3
Dartmouth Terrace 28 D3
David Park 11 B1
David Road 11 B1
Davis Place 19 B3[2]
Davitt Road 25 A1
Dawson Lane 20 D3
Dawson Street 20 D3
De Velara Place 12 C2[9]
De Burgh Road 18 C2[1]
De Courcy Square 3 B3
Dean Street 27 B1
Dean Swift Square 19 A3
Delvin Road 10 D1
Delvin Terrace 11 B3[16]
Demesne 8 C2
Denmark St Great 12 C3
Denzille Lane 21 A3
Dermot O'Hurley Ave 22 D3
Derrynane Gardens 22 D3
Derrynane Parade 12 C2[3]
Desmond Street 27 B2
Deverell Place 20 D1[6]
Devery's Lane 11 B1
Devlin's Place 21 A3
Devoy Road 25 A1
Dexter Terrace 28 D3[1]
Digges Lane 20 C3

Digges St Upr 28 C1
Dillon Place South 19 B3
Dingle Road 9 B1
Distillery Road 13 A1
Dodder Terrace 22 D3
Dodder View Cotts 30 C2⁵
Dolphin Avenue 26 D2
Dolphin House 26 C2
Dolphin Park 25 B2
Dolphin Road 25 B2
Dolphin's Barn 26 C2
Dolphin's Barn St 26 C2
Dominick Lane 19 B1
Dominick Place 20 C1
Dominick St Lwr 19 B1
Dominick St Upr 11 B3
Donelan Avenue 18 C3
Donnycarney 6 D1
Donnycarney Road 6 D2
Donore Avenue 26 D1
Donore Road 26 D1
Donore Terrace 26 D1
Donovan Lane 27 A2
Doon Avenue 10 C2
Doris Street 22 C3
Dorset Lane 12 C2
Dorset Place 12 C2
Dorset Street Lwr 12 C2
Dorset Street Upr 11 B3
Dowling's Court 21 A2
Downpatrick Road 25 B3
Dowth Avenue 10 D1
Dromard Terrace 31 A1
Drumalee Avenue 10 C3
Drumalee Court 10 C3
Drumalee Drive 10 C3
Drumalee Grove 10 C3
Drumalee Park 10 C3
Drumalee Road 10 C3
Drumcliffe Road 9 B1
Drumcliffe Drive 10 C1
Drumcondra 4 D2
Drumcondra Park 12 D2¹
Drumcondra Rd Lwr 4 D3/12 C1
Drumcondra Rd Upr 4 D3
Drummond Place 27 B3⁴
Drury Street 20 C3
Dufferin Avenue 27 A2
Duke Lane Lower 20 C3
Duke Lane Upper 20 C3
Duke Row 13 A3⁴
Duke Street 20 C3
Dunard Avenue 9 A2
Dunard Court 9 B2
Dunard Drive 9 B2
Dunard Park 9 B2

Dunard Road 9 B2
Dunard Walk 9 B2
Duncan Court 8 D3¹
Dunluce Road 8 C2
Dunmanus Road 9 B1
Dunne Street 13 A3
Dunseverick Road 7 B3
Durham Road 31 B2
Earl Street North 20 C1
Earl Street South 19 A3
Earl Place 20 C1
Earls Court 9 B2
Earlsfort Terrace 28 D2
East Road 22 C1
East Road 14 C3
  (East Wall)
East Wall 14 C3
East Wall Road 14 C2
East Wall Rd 22 D1
  (North Wall)
Eastmoreland La 29 B2
Eastmoreland Pl 29 B2¹
Ebenezer Terrace 26 C1
Eblana Villas 21 B3
Eccles Court 12 C2
Eccles Place 12 C2
Eccles Street 11 B2
Echlin Street 18 D3
Eden Quay 20 D2
Edgewood 4 D3¹
Elgin Road 29 B2
Elizabeth Street 12 D1
Ellesmere Avenue 10 C2
Ellford Terrace 26 D2³
Ellis Court 18 D2⁶
Ellis Quay 18 D2
Ellis Street 18 D2
Elm Mount Avenue 6 D1
Elm Mount Court 7 A1
Elm Mount Drive 7 A1
Elm Mount Road 7 A1
Elm Road 6 D1
Ely Place 28 D1
Ely Place Upper 28 D1²
Emerald Cottages 30 C1²
Emerald Place 21 A1
Emerald Square 26 C1
Emerald Street 21 B1
Emerald Terrace 26 D1
Emmet Street 12 D2
  (Inchicore)
Emmet Street 27 A3
  (Harold's Cross)
Emmet Road 17 A3
Emor Street 27 B2
Emorville Avenue 27 B2

Empress Place 13 A3
Engine Alley 19 A3¹⁷
Ennafort Court 8 D1
Ennafort Park 8 D1
Ennafort Road 8 D1
Ennaville Road 13 B2
Ennis Grove 30 D1
Enniskerry Road 11 B1
Erne Place 21 A3
Erne Place Little 21 A3
Erne Place Lower 21 A2
Erne Street Lower 21 A2
Erne Street Upper 21 A3
Erne Terrace Front 21 A3
Erne Terrace Rere 21 A3
Erris Road 10 C1
Esmond Avenue 13 B1
Essex Gate 19 B2¹
Essex Quay 19 B2
Essex Street E 20 C2
Essex Street W 19 B2
Estate Cottages 29 B1
Estate Cottages 30 C2⁶
  (Ballsbridge)
Eugene Street 26 D1
Eustace Street 20 C2
Everton Avenue 10 C2
Ewington Lane 18 C3
Exchange St Lwr 19 B2
Exchange St Upr 19 B2²
Exchequer Street 20 C3
Fade Street 20 C3
Fairfield Avenue 13 B3
Fairfield Road 3 B3
Fairview 14 C1
Fairview Ave Lwr 13 B1
Fairview Ave Upr 14 C1
Fairview Green 13 B1
Fairview Passage 13 B1
Fairview Strand 13 B1
Fairview Terrace 13 B1
Faith Avenue 13 B2
Farney Park 31 A2
Father Matthew Sq 19 A1⁴
Father Scully Hse 12 D3¹⁷
Fatima Mansions 26 C1³
Faussagh Avenue 1 B3
Faussagh Road 10 D1
Fenian Street 21 A3
Ferguson Road 4 C2
Ferrymans Crossing 21 B1³
Fertullagh Road 10 D1¹
Findlater Place 20 C1¹
Findlater Street 18 C1
Fingal Place 10 D3
Fingal Street 26 D1

Finglas Road 2 D2
Finglas Road Old 2 D1
Finn Street 18 C1
First Avenue 21 B1
Fishamble Street 19 B2
Fisherman's Wharf 22 D2[1]
Fitzgerald Street 27 B3[2]
Fitzgibbon Lane 12 D2
Fitzgibbon Street 12 D2
Fitzroy Avenue 12 D1
Fitzwilliam Court 28 D1[1]
Fitzwilliam Lane 29 A1
Fitzwilliam Place 28 D2
Fitzwilliam Pl Little 29 A1[3]
Fitzwilliam Pl Nth 19 A1[1]
Fitzwilliam Quay 22 D3
Fitzwilliam Sq E 29 A1
Fitzwilliam Sq N 29 A1
Fitzwilliam Sq S 28 D1
Fitzwilliam Sq W 28 D1
Fitzwilliam Street 22 D3
Fitzwilliam St. Lwr 29 A1
Fitzwilliam St. Upr. 29 A1
Flag Alley 19 A3[16]
Fleet Street 20 C2
Fleming Road 4 C2
Fleming's Place 29 A2
Florence Street 27 B2[4]
Foley Street 20 D1
Fontenoy Street 11 B3
Forbes Lane 26 D1
Forbes Street 21 B2
Forth Road 14 C3
Fortview Avenue 16 D2
Foster Place North 13 A2[11]
Foster Place South 20 C2
Foster Terrace 13 A2
Fountain Place 19 A1
Fountain Road 17 B1
Fourth Avenue 21 B1
Fownes St Lwr 20 C2[7]
Fownes St Upr 20 C2
Foyle Road 5 B3
Francis Street 19 A3
Frankfort Cottages 13 A3
Frederick Court 12 C3[4]
Frederick Lane N 12 C3[7]
Frederick Lane S 20 D3
Frederick St Nth 12 C3
Frederick St Sth 20 D3
French Mullen Flats 28 C2[8]
Frenchman's Lane 20 D1[1]
Friary Avenue 19 A1
Friary Grove 19 A1[7]
Fumbally Lane 27 B1
Furry Park Court 8 C2

Furry Park Road 8 C2
Gaelic Street 13 B3
Galmoy Road 10 D1
Galtymore Drive 25 A2
Galtymore Road 25 A2
Garda Terrace 18 C1
Garden Lane 19 A3
Garden Terrace 27 A2[6]
Garden View 28 C3[5]
Gardiner Lane 12 D3
Gardiner Place 12 C3
Gardiner Row 12 C3[5]
Gardiner St Lwr 20 D1
Gardiner St Mid 12 D3
Gardiner St Upr 12 C2
Gartan Avenue 12 C1
Geoffrey Keating Rd 27 A1[3]
George Reynolds Flats 22 D3[17]
George's Hill 19 B1
George's Lane 19 A1
George's Place 12 C2[12]
George's Wharf 11 B2[14]
George's St Gt N 12 C3
George's St Gt S 20 C3
George's Quay 20 D2
Gerald Street 22 C3
Geraldine Street 11 B2
Gilbert Road 27 A2
Gilford Avenue 31 B3
Gilford Court 31 A2
Gilford Drive 31 A3
Gilford Park 31 A3
Gilford Road 31 A2
Gilford Terrace 31 B3
Glandore Road 5 B2
Glasnevin 3 B2
Glasnevin Court 2 C1
Glasnevin Downs 2 D1
Glasnevin Hill 3 B2
Glasnevin Oaks 2 D1
Glasnevin Woods 2 C1
Glenard Avenue 10 C2
Glenarm Avenue 4 D3
Glenbeigh Park 9 B2
Glenbeigh Road 10 C2
Glencar Road 9 B3
Glendalough Road 4 C3
Glendinning Lane 20 C3[10]
Glenealy Road 26 C3
Glengarriff Parade 12 C2
Glenmalure Park 25 B1
Glenmore Road 9 B2
Gloucester Diamond 12 D3[13]
Gloucester Lane 12 D3[8]
Gloucester Pl Lwr 12 D3[9]
Gloucester Pl Upr 12 D3

Gloucester St Sth 21 A2
Glovers Alley 20 C3
Glovers Court 20 C3[16]
Godfrey Place 10 C3
Golden Lane 19 B3
Goldenbridge Ave 25 A1
Goldsmith Street 11 B2
Gordon Place 28 C2[5]
Gordon Street 22 C3
Gortbeg Avenue 1 B1
Gortbeg Drive 1 B1
Gortbeg Park 1 B1
Gortbeg Road 1 B1
Gortmore Park 1 B1
Grace Park Avenue 5 A3
Grace Pk Gardens 5 A3
Grace Park Heights 5 B1
Grace Pk Meadows 6 C1
Grace Park Road 5 B1
Grace Park Terrace 5 B2
Gracefield Avenue 8 D1
Grafton Street 20 C3
Graham's Row 11 B3[5]
Granby Lane 11 B3
Granby Place 20 C1
Granby Row 11 B3
Grand Canal Quay 21 B3
Grand Canal St Lwr 21 B3
Grand Canal St Upr 29 B1
Grand Canal View 25 A1
Grand Canal Place 18 D3
Grand Parade 28 D2
Grangegorman Lwr 19 A1
Grangegorman Upr 11 A3
Grangegorman Villas 11 A3[2]
Granite Place 30 C3[3]
Grant's Row 21 A3
Grantham Place 28 C2
Grantham Street 27 B2
Grattan Court East 29 B1[3]
Grattan Hall 29 B1[7]
Grattan Parade 12 C1
Grattan Place 21 B3
Gray Square 19 A3[2]
Gray Street 19 A3
Great Western Ave 11 A2
Great Western Sq 11 A2
Great Western Villas 11 A2
Greek Street 19 B2
Green Street 19 B1
Green Street East 22 C2
Green Street Little 19 B1
Greenfield Place 27 B3[1]
Greenmount Ave 27 A3
Greenmount Court 27 A3
Greenmount Lane 27 A3

Greenmount Square	27 A3²	Hardwicke Lane	12 C3³	Hogan Place	21 A3
Greenore Terrace	21 B3²	Hardwicke Place	12 C3⁶	Holles Place	21 A3
Greenville	27 A2⁷	Hardwicke Street	12 C3	Holles Row	21 A3
Greenville Avenue	27 A2	Harman Street	26 D1	Holles Street	21 A3
Greenville Parade	27 A2¹	Harmony Row	21 A3	Holly Road	6 D2
Greenville Terrace	27 A2	Harold Road	18 D1	Hollybank Road	4 C3
Grenville Lane	12 C3	Harolds Cross	26 D3	Hollybrook Court	15 A1³
Grenville Street	12 C3	Harolds Cross Cotts	27 A3⁵	Hollybrook Ct Dr	15 A1²
Griffith Avenue	3 A1	Harolds Cross Rd	27 A3	Hollybrook Grove	14 D1
(Finglas)		Haroldville Avenue	26 C1	Hollybrook Park	7 A3
Griffith Avenue	5 B2	Harrington Street	27 B2	Hollybrook Road	15 A1
(Marino)		Harry Court	27 B1⁷	Holycross Avenue	12 D1
Griffith Avenue	4 C1	Harry Street	20 C3¹	Holyrood Park	31 A3
(Whitehall)		Harty Place	27 B1	Home Farm Park	4 D2
Griffith Court	5 B3	Hastings Street	22 C3	Home Farm Road	4 C1
Griffith Downs	5 A1	Hatch Lane	28 D2	Homelee	30 D2³
Griffith Lawns	4 C1	Hatch Place	28 D2	Hope Avenue	13 B2
Griffith Square	27 A2⁵	Hatch Street Lower	28 D2	Hope Street	22 C3
Grosvenor Court	8 C3	Hatch Street Upper	28 C2	Hospital Lane	17 A2³
Grove Avenue	27 B3⁵	Hatters Lane	27 A3¹	Hotel Yard	20 C1
Grove Park	27 B3	Havelock Square	30 C1	Houghton Terrace	18 D1¹
Grove Road	27 B3	Havelock Terrace	30 D1¹	Howard Street	22 C3
Guild Street	21 B1	Haverty Road	14 C1	Howth Rd	7 B3
Guildford Place	13 A3¹	Hawkins Street	20 D2	(Clontarf)	
Haddington Place	29 B1	Hawthorn Avenue	13 B3	Howth Rd	6 D3
Haddington Road	29 B1	Hawthorn Terrace	13 B3	(Fairview)	
Haddon Court	15 B2²	Haymarket	19 A2	Howth Rd	8 C2
Haddon Park	15 A1	Hazel Road	6 D1	(Killester)	
Haddon Road	15 B1	Healy Street	12 D3	Hume Street	28 D1
Hagan's Court	29 A1	Hendrick Lane	18 D2⁵	Huxley Crescent	26 D1²
Halliday Road	18 D1	Hendrick Place	18 D2²	Hyacinth Street	13 B3
Halliday Square	18 C1	Henrietta House	19 B1⁵	Hybreasal	25 A1¹
Halpin's Row	13 A3¹¹	Henrietta Lane	11 B3	Imaal Road	10 D2
Halston Street	19 B1	Henrietta Place	19 B1	Inchicore Road	17 B3
Hamilton Court	19 B2⁵	Henrietta Street	19 B1	Infirmary Road	17 B1
Hamilton Street	26 D1	Henry Place	20 C1	Ingram Road	27 A2
Hammond Lane	19 A2	Henry Street	20 C1	Innisfallen Parade	12 C2
Hammond Street	27 A1	Hepenstal Terrace	31 B2¹	Inns Quay	19 A2
Hampstead Park	4 C1	Herbert Cottages	30 C2⁴	Inver Road	9 B1
Hampton Court	29 B3⁴	Herbert Lane	29 A1	Inverness Road	13 B1
Hampton Estate	8 D3	Herbert Park	30 C3	Iona Crescent	3 B3
Hampton Green	9 A1	Herbert Park Lane	30 C3	Iona Drive	4 C3
Hanbury Lane	19 A3	Herbert Place	29 A1	Iona Park	3 B3
Hanover Court	19 B3¹⁴	(Baggot Street)		Iona Road	3 B3
Hanover Lane	19 B3	Herbert Place	22 D3⁴	Iona Villas	4 C3
Hanover Quay	22 C2	(Irishtown)		Irishtown	31 A1
Hanover Square	19 B3	Herbert Road	30 D2	Irishtown Road	22 D3
Hanover St E	21 A2	Herbert Street	29 A1	Irvine Cottages	22 C1²
Hanover St W	19 A3⁹	Herberton Drive	26 C2	Irvine Terrace	22 C1
Harbour Court	20 D1	Herberton Park	25 B2	Irwin Court	17 B3³
Harcourt Lane	28 C2¹⁰	Herberton Road	25 B1	Irwin Street	17 B3⁴
Harcourt Road	28 C2	Heytesbury Street	27 B2	Island Street	18 D2
Harcourt Street	28 C1	Heytesbury Lane	29 B3	Island Villa	21 B3¹
Harcourt Terrace	28 D2	Hibernian Avenue	13 B3	Islandbridge	17 A2
Hardiman Road	4 C2	High Street	19 B3	Islandbridge Court	17 A2²
Hardwicke Arch	12 C3²	Hill Street	12 C3	Isolda Road	23 A3

51

Name	Ref	Name	Ref	Name	Ref
Ivar Street	18 D1	Kinahan Street	18 C1	Leinster Avenue	13 B2
Iveagh Buildings (Bride Rd)	19 B3[11]	Kincora Avenue	15 B1	Leinster Lane	20 D3
Iveagh Buildings (Kevin St Upr)	27 B1[3]	Kincora Drive	15 B1	Leinster Market	20 D2[6]
Iveagh Gardens	25 A3	Kincora Grove	15 B1	Leinster Street E	13 B2[5]
Ivetta Terrace	4 D3[3]	Kincora Park	16 C1	Leinster Street N	11 A1
Ivy Terrace	26 D1	Kincora Road	16 C1	Leinster Street S	20 D3
James's Place E	29 A1	King Street North	19 A1	Leitrim Place	29 B7
James's Street	18 C3	King Street South	20 C3	Leix Road	10 D2
James's Street E	29 A1	King's Avenue	13 A2[16]	Leland Place	21 A1
James's Street N	13 B2[6]	Kingram Place	28 D2	Lemon Street	20 C3
Janeville	27 B2[7]	Kings Inns Court	11 B3[13]	Lennox Place	27 B2
Jervis Lane Lower	19 B2	Kings Court	10 D3[3]	Lennox Street	28 C2
Jervis Lane Upper	19 B1	Kingsland Pk Ave	28 D2[3]	Lennox Terrace	28 C2[12]
Jervis Street	19 B1	Kingsland Parade	27 B3	Leo Avenue	12 C2[11]
John Dillon Street	19 B3	Kippure Park	1 A1	Leo Street	12 C2
John Field Road	19 B3[6]	Kirkwood	31 A3	Leslie's Building	11 A2
John Street South	27 A1	Kirwan Street	18 D1	Leukos Road	23 A3
John Street West	19 A3	Kirwan St Cotts	10 D3	Liberty House	12 D3[11]
John's Lane	19 A3	Knightsbridge	15 B1[3]	Liberty Lane	28 C1
John's Lane East	19 B3	Knocknarea Avenue	25 A3	Liberty Square	19 A3[12]
John's Street North	18 D2[4]	Knocknarrow Tce	17 B3[11]	Library View Tce	11 B2[1]
Johnson Court	20 C3	Kyle-Clare Road	23 A3[1]	Liffey Street Lower	20 C2
Johnson Place	20 C3[12]	La Vista Avenue	7 B1	Liffey Street Upper	20 C1
Jones's Road	12 D2	Lad Lane	29 A1	Liffey Street West	18 D2
Josephine Avenue	12 C2[10]	Lad Lane Upper	29 A2	Lime Street	21 A2
Joy Street	22 C3	Lady's Lane	17 A3	Limekiln Avenue	27 A3
Joyce Road	4 C2	Lagan Road	1 B1	Lincoln Lane	19 A2[3]
Kearn's Place	17 A3[4]	Lamb Alley	19 A3	Lincoln Place	20 D3
Keeper Road	25 B2	Lambay Road	4 C1	Lindsay Road	11 B1
Kelly's Lane	11 B2[8]	Lambourne Village	15 B1[4]	Linenhall Parade	19 B1
Kelly's Row	12 C2	Langan Road	2 B2	Linenhall Street	19 B1[4]
Kenmare Parade	12 C2[1]	Langrishe Place	12 D3[15]	Linenhall Terrace	19 B1
Kerlogue Road	23 A3	Lansdowne Cres	30 C1[4]	Lisburn Street	19 B1
Kevin Street Lower	27 B1	Lansdowne Gdns	30 C2[2]	Liscannor Road	1 B3
Kevin Street Upper	27 B1	Lansdowne Hall	30 D1[2]	Lissadel Avenue	25 A3
Kevin Barry Flats	19 A1[8]	Lansdowne Lane	30 C1	Lissadel Court	25 A3
Kevins Avenue	27 B1[2]	Lansdowne Park	30 C1	Lissadel Drive	25 A2
Kickham Road	25 A1	Lansdowne Road	30 C2	Lissenfield	29 C3[2]
Kilbride Road	7 B2	Lansdowne Terrace	30 C1[1]	Little Britain Street	19 B1
Kildare Place	20 D3[3]	Lansdowne Village	30 D1	Little Mary Street	19 B2
Kildare Street	20 D3	Lansdowne Villas	30 C1[3]	Litton Lane	20 C2[1]
Kilkiernan Court	1 B3	Lawrence Grove	7 A3	Lombard Street E	21 A2
Kilkieran Road	1 B3	Le Vere Terrace	27 A3[4]	Lombard Street W	27 B2
Killala Road	1 B3	Lea Crescent	31 B2	Lombard Court	21 A2[3]
Killan Road	22 C1	Lea Road	31 B2	Lomond Avenue	5 B3
Killarney Avenue	13 A3[7]	Leahy's Terrace	31 A1	Londonbridge Drive	30 D1
Killarney Parade	12 C2	Lee Road	2 C2	Londonbridge Road	30 D1
Killarney Street	13 A3	Leeson Close	28 D2	Long Lane	11 B3
Killester	8 C1	Leeson Lane	28 D1	Long Lane Close	27 B1[9]
Killester Avenue	7 A1/7 B2	Leeson Park	29 A3	Long's Place	18 D3
Killester Park	7 B1	Leeson Park Ave	29 A3	Longford Lane	20 C3[8]
Kilmainham	17 A3	Leeson Place	28 D2	Longford St Great	19 B3[7]
Kilmainham Lane	17 B3	Leeson Street Lwr	28 D1	Longford St Little	20 C3[7]
Kilmainham Village	18 C3[2]	Leeson Street Upr	29 A2	Longwood Avenue	27 B2
		Leeson Village	29 A3	Lord Edward Court	19 B3[12]
		Leeson Walk	28 D3	Lord Edward Street	19 B3

Lord's Walk	9 A3	Marlborough Mews	10 C3	Mespil Road	29 A2
Loreto Road	26 D1	Marlborough Place	20 D1⁴	Middle Third	8 C1
Lorne Terrace	17 B3¹⁴	Marlborough Road	10 C3	Military Road	17 B3
Lotts	20 C2	Marlborough Street	20 C1	(Kilmainham)	
Lourdes House	12 D3¹⁴	Marmion Court	19 A1⁶	Military Rd	28 C3
Lourdes Road	26 C1	Marne Villas	11 A3	(Rathmines)	
Love Lane East	29 B1²	Marrowbone Lane	18 D3	Mill Brook	17 B3¹⁵
Luby Road	17 A3	Marrowbone La Blds	18 D3³	Mill Lane	27 A1
Luke Street	20 D2	Marrowbone La Clo	26 D1⁵	Mill Street	27 A1
Lullymore Terrace	26 D2	Marshal Lane	18 D2	Millbourne Avenue	4 C3
Lurgan Street	19 B1¹¹	Marshalsea Lane	18 D3²	Millbrook Terrace	17 A3⁷
Lynch's Place	11 B2⁵	Martello View	31 B2	Millmount Avenue	4 C3
Lynton Court	30 D3²	Martin Street	27 A1	Millmount Place	4 D3
Mabel Street	12 D1	Martin White Chalets	30 D2²	Millmount Terrace	4 D3
Mabbot Lane	20 D1	Mary Aikenhead Ho	18 C3⁴	Millmount Villas	4 C3
Macken Street	21 B3	Mary's Abbey	19 B2	Misery Hill	21 B2
Macken Villa	21 B3	Mary's Lane	19 B2	Mitchell House	29 A3³
Mackie's Place	28 D1	Matt Talbot Court	12 D3¹	Moira Road	18 C1
Mackie's Place	28 D1¹³	Mauncell Place	11 B3¹⁴	Moland Place	20 D1²
Madden Road	27 A1	Maxwell Street	26 D1	Molesworth Place	20 D3²
Madison Road	25 B1	May Lane	19 A2	Molesworth Street	20 D3
Magdalen Terrace	22 D3⁷	May Park	7 A1	Molyneux Yard	19 A3
Magennis Place	21 A2	May Street	12 D2	Monck Place	11 A2
Magennis Square	21 A2¹	Mayfield Road	25 B1	Montague Place	28 C1
Malachi Place	13 B3¹	Mayor Street Lower	21 A1	Montague Court	28 C1¹³
Malachi Road	18 D1	Mayor Street Upper	22 C1	Montague Lane	28 C1
Malahide Rd	7 A1	Mc Dowell Avenue	18 C3¹	Montague Street	28 C1
(Donnycarney)		McCarthy Terrace	26 C1¹	Montpelier Drive	18 C1
Malahide Rd	14 C1	McKee Park	9 B2	Montpelier Gardens	18 C1²
(Fairview)		McMahon Street	27 B2	Montpelier Hill	18 C1
Malahide Rd	6 D3	Meades Terrace	21 A3	Montpelier Park	18 C1
(Marino)		Meath Market	19 A3¹³	Moore Lane	20 C1
Mallin Avenue	26 C1	Meath Place	19 A3	Moore Street	20 C1
Malone Gardens	30 C1	Meath Square	19 A3³	Moracrete Cotts	25 B3¹
Malpas Street	27 A1	Meetinghouse Lane	19 B2³	Morehampton Lane	29 B3
Malpas Terrace	27 B1	Melrose Avenue	13 B1	Morehampton Mews	29 B3²
Mander's Terrace	28 D3³	Memorial Road	20 D1	Morehampton Sq	29 B3¹
Mannix Road	4 C3	Mercer Street Lwr	20 C3	Morgan Place	19 A2⁴
Manor Place	18 D1	Mercer Street Upr	28 C1	Morning Star Ave	19 A1
Manor Street	18 D1	Merchamp	16 D1	Morning Star Road	26 C1
Malpas Court	27 B1⁴	Merchant's Arch	20 C2⁶	Morrogh Terrace	5 B2¹
Margaret Place	30 C1	Merchant's Quay	19 A2	Moss Street	20 D2
Marguerite Road	3 B3	Merchant's Road	14 D3	Mount Brown	17 B3
Marine Drive	31 A2	Merrion Close	21 A3²	Mount Drummond	27 A3
Marino	5 B3	Merrion Place	20 D3	Avenue	
Marino Avenue	6 D3	Merrion Road	30 D3	Mount Drummond	27 B3
Marino Crescent	14 C1	Merrion Row	28 D1	Square	
Marino Green	6 C3	Merrion Sq E	29 A1	Mount Prospect Lwr	8 D3
Marino Mart	14 C1	Merrion Sq N	21 A3	Mount St Cres	29 B1⁴
Marino Park	6 C3	Merrion Sq S	29 A1	Mount St Lower	29 B1
Marino Park Ave	14 C1	Merrion Sq W	21 A3	Mount St Upper	29 A1
Marion Villas	26 D1	Merrion St Lwr	21 A3	Mount Temple Rd	18 D1
Mark's Alley West	19 A3	Merrion St Upr	28 D1	Mountain View Ct	12 D3¹⁸
Mark's Lane	21 A2	Merton Avenue	27 A2	Mountjoy Parade	12 D2¹⁴
Market Street South	18 D3	Merton Park	27 A2	Mountjoy Place	12 D3
Marks Street	20 D2	Merville Avenue	14 C1	Mountjoy Sq E	12 D3
				Mountjoy Sq N	12 D2

Mountjoy Sq S	12 D3	North Wall	21 B1	Oriel Place	13 B3
Mountjoy Sq W	12 C3	North Wall Quay	21 B2	Oriel Street Lower	13 B3
Mountjoy Street	11 B3	Northbrook Avenue	28 D3	Oriel Street Upper	21 A1
Mountjoy St Mid	11 B3[9]	Northbrook Ave Lwr	13 B2	Ormeau Street	22 C3[1]
Mountpleasant Ave Lwr	28 C3	Northbrook Ave Upr	13 B2	Ormond Place	19 B2[4]
Mountpleasant Ave Upr	28 C3	Northbrook Lane	28 D3	Ormond Quay Lwr	20 C2
Mountpleasant Pde	28 C3[6]	Northbrook Road	28 D3	Ormond Quay Upr	19 B2
Mountpleasant Pl	28 D3[2]	Northbrook Terrace	13 B2[7]	Ormond Road	4 D3
Mountpleasant Sq	28 C3	Northland Drive	2 D1	Ormond Square	19 B2
Mountpleasant Tce	28 C3	Northland Grove	2 D1	Ormond Street	27 A1
Mountpleasant Tce Upr	28 C3[8]	Northumberland Rd	29 B1	Osbourne Terrace	28 D3[8]
Mountpleasant Villas	28 D3[4]	Northumberland Sq	20 D1[5]	Oscar Square	27 A1
Mountshannon Rd	25 B1	Norton's Avenue	11 A2	Ossory Road	13 B3
Mourne Rd	25 A2	Nottingham Street	13 B2	Ostman Place	18 D1
Moy Elta Road	13 B3	O'Brien's Place N	4 C2	Oswald Road	31 A1
Moyle Road	2 C2	O'Brien's Terrace	11 B1	Oulton Park	16 C1
Muckross Parade	12 C2[2]	O'Carolan Road	27 A1	Our Lady's Close	26 D1[6]
Mullinahack	19 A2[9]	O'Connell Avenue	11 B2	Our Lady's Rd	26 D1
Mulroy Road	2 C3	O'Connell Gardens	30 D1	Ovoca Road	27 B2
Munster Street	11 A1	O'Connell St Upr	20 C1	Owens Avenue	17 B3[7]
Murtagh Road	18 D1	O'Connell St Lwr	20 C1	Oxford Road	28 D3
Myrtle Street	11 B3	O'Curry Avenue	27 A1[5]	Oxmantown Lane	19 A2
Nassau Place	20 D3[1]	O'Curry Road	27 A1	Oxmantown Road	10 C3
Navan Road	9 A1	O'Daly Road	4 C2	Palace Street	20 C2[12]
Nassau Street	20 D3	O'Devaney Gardens	18 C1	Palatine Square	18 C1
Nelson Street	11 B2	O'Donovan Road	27 A2	Palmerston Place	11 B3
Nephin Road	9 A1	O'Hara Avenue	27 B3	Paradise Place	11 B3
Nerney's Court	12 C3	O'Leary Road	25 A1	Park Avenue	31 A3
New Bride Street	27 B1	O'Neachtain Road	4 C2[1]	Park Avenue West	18 C2[2]
New Ireland Road	25 B1	O'Neill's Buildings	28 C1[4]	Park Court	31 A3
New Row South	27 A1	O'Quinn Avenue	18 C3	Park Lane	31 A3
New Row Square	27 A1	O'Rahilly House	22 D3[11]	Park Lane East	20 D2
New Street North	19 A1	O'Rahilly Parade	20 C1	Park Place	17 A2[1]
New Street Grdns	27 B1[8]	O'Reilly Avenue	17 B3	Park Terrace	19 A3[10]
New Street South	27 B1	O'Sullivan Avenue	13 A2	Park View	9 B2
New Wapping St	22 C1	Oak Road	6 D2	Parkgate Street	18 C2
Newbridge Avenue	30 D1	Oakfield Place	27 B2	Parkview Court	9 A2[1]
Newbridge Drive	30 D1	Oaklands Drive	31 A2	Parkview Place	22 D3[3]
Newcomen Avenue	13 A2	Oaklands Park	30 D2	Parliament Row	20 C2[10]
Newcomen Court	13 A2[7]	Oakley Park	8 D3	Parliament Street	19 B2
Newgrange Road	10 D1	Observatory Lane	28 C3[1]	Parnell Avenue	27 A3
Newgrove Avenue	31 B2	Offaly Road	10 D1	Parnell Court	27 A3
Newmarket	27 A1	Olaf Road	18 D1	Parnell Place	12 C3
Newmarket Street	27 A1	Old Cabra Road	10 C2	Parnell Road	26 D2
Newport Street	18 D3	Old County Road	25 B3	Parnell Sq East	12 C3
Niall Street	10 C3	Old Kilmainham	17 B3	Parnell Sq North	12 C3
Nicholas Avenue	19 A1	Old Mill Court	27 B1[1]	Parnell Sq West	12 C3
Nicholas Street	19 B3	Old Mountpleasant	28 D3	Parnell Street	12 C3/20 C
Nore Road	2 C2	Old County Glen	25 B3	Patrick Street	19 B3
Norfolk Road	11 A1	Oliver Plunkett Ave	22 D3	Pearse Grove	21 B3[4]
Norseman Place	18 D1	Oliver Bond Street	19 A2	Pearse House	21 A2
North Circular Road	10 C3	Oliver Bond House	19 A2[6]	Pearse Square	21 B2
North Circular Road	12 D2	Ontario Terrace	28 C3	Pearse Street	20 D2
North Quay Ext	22 D2	Orchard Lane	28 D3	Pembroke Cottages	22 D2
North Road	9 A2	Orchard Road	13 A1	Pembroke Gardens	29 B2
North Strand Road	13 A3	Orchard View	11 A3[1]	Pembroke Lane	29 A1

Pembroke Park	29 B3
Pembroke Place	28 D2²
Pembroke Place (Ballsbridge)	30 C3²
Pembroke Road	29 B2
Pembroke Road	30 C1
Pembroke Row	29 A1
Pembroke Street	22 D3
Pembroke St Lwr	28 D1
Pembroke St Upr	28 D1
Penrose Street	22 C3
Percy Lane	29 B1
Percy Place	29 B1
Peter Place	28 C2
Peter Row	28 C1
Peter Street	19 B3
Peterson's Court	21 A2²
Petrie Road	27 A2
Phibsboro	11 A2
Phibsborough	11 B2
Phibsborough Ave	11 A2
Phibsborough Place	11 B2⁷
Phibsborough Road	11 B2
Philipsburgh Ave	5 B3/13 B1
Philipsburgh Terrace	5 B3
Philomena Terrace	22 D3⁵
Phoenix Court	18 C1
Phoenix Manor	10 C3
Phoenix Street N	19 A2
Pig Lane	12 D3
Pigeon House Road	24 C3
Pigeon House Rd (Ringsend)	23 A2
Pim Street	18 D3
Pimlico	19 A3
Pimlico Cottages	19 A3¹⁸
Pine Hurst	9 B1
Pine Road	23 A3
Pleasants Lane	28 C1
Pleasants Place	28 C1
Pleasant's Street	27 B1
Polo Road	9 A3
Poolbeg Street	20 D2
Poole Street	19 A3¹⁹
Poplar Row	13 B2
Poplar Row (Apts)	13 B2⁴
Portland Close	13 A3⁵
Portland Court	12 D2³
Portland Place	12 C2
Portland Row	13 A3
Portland Square	12 D2⁸
Portland Street N	12 D2
Portland Street W	18 D3
Portmahon Drive	25 B1
Portobello Harbour	28 C2
Portobello Place	28 C2¹³
Portobello Road	27 B3
Power's Court	29 B1
Power's Square	19 B3¹⁵
Prebend Street	19 A1
Preston Street	13 A3⁸
Price's Lane (Aston's Qy)	20 C2
Price's Lane (Ranelagh)	28 C3
Priestfield Cottages	26 D2¹
Priestfield Drive	26 D2²
Primrose Avenue	11 B3
Primrose Street	11 B3³
Prince of Wales Tce	30 D3¹
Prince's St Sth	21 A2
Prince's St Nth	20 C1
Prior Hall	18 C3³
Proby's Lane	20 C1
Promenade Road	15 A3
Prospect Avenue	3 B3
Prospect Road	11 B1
Prospect Square	3 B3
Prospect Terrace (Kilmainham)	17 A3⁶
Prospect Terrace (Sandymount)	31 A1⁴
Prospect Way	3 B3
Protestant Row	28 C1²
Proud's Lane	28 C1
Prussia Street	10 D3
Pyro Villas	26 D1
Quarry Cottages	7 B2¹
Quarry Road	10 C1
Queen Street	19 A2
Quinn's Lane	28 D1
Raglan Lane	29 B2
Raglan Road	29 B2
Railway Street	12 D3
Railway Cottages	30 D2¹
Rainsford Street	18 D3
Railway Terrace	21 B3
Rainsford Avenue	18 D3¹
Raleigh Square	25 A3
Ranelagh	28 D3
Ranelagh Avenue	28 D3
Rath Row	20 D2²
Rathdown Road	11 A2
Rathdown Square	10 D3
Rathdown Road	26 C3
Rathlin Road	4 C1
Rathmines	27 C3
Rathmines Rd Lwr	28 C3
Ratoath Estate	1 A2
Ratoath Road	1 A2
Ravensdale Road	14 C3
Raymond Street	27 A2
Red Cow Lane	19 A1
Redmond's Hill	28 C1
Reginald Square	19 A3⁴
Reginald Street	19 A3
Rehoboth Avenue	26 D2
Rehoboth Place	26 C2
Reilly's Avenue	26 C2
Reuben Avenue	26 C1
Reuben Street	26 C1
Rialto Buildings	26 C1
Rialto Cottages	25 B1
Rialto Drive	25 B2
Rialto Place	26 C1⁴
Rialto Street	26 C1
Richmond Avenue	13 A1
Richmond Cottages	13 A2³
Richmond Cotts N	13 A2³
Richmond Crescent	13 A2²
Richmond Estate	13 B1
Richmond Hill	28 C3
Richmond Lane	12 D2¹²
Richmond Mews	28 C3
Richmond Parade	13 A2¹⁰
Richmond Place	28 C3
Richmond Pl Sth	28 C2⁹
Richmond Road	4 D3/13 A1
Richmond Row	28 C2
Richmond St Nth	13 A2
Richmond St Sth	28 C2
Richmond Villas	28 C2⁴
Ringsend	22 D3
Ringsend Park	22 D2
Ringsend Road	22 C3
River Gardens	3 B2
Riverston Abbey	1 A2
Robert Place	12 D1¹
Robert Street	18 D3
Robert Street (Drumcondra)	12 D1
Robert Street South	18 D3
Roger's Lane	28 D1
Roosevelt Cottages	9 A1
Rope Walk Place	22 D3
Rosary Road	26 C1
Rosary Terrace	22 D3
Rosedale Terrace	27 B2²
Rosemount	7 A1
Rosemount Court	17 A3¹
Rosemount Road	11 A2
Rosemount Terrace	18 D1
Rosevale Court	8 D1
Rosevale Mansions	8 D1
Ross Street	10 C3
Ross Road	19 B3
Rostrevor Terrace	21 B3³
Rothe Abbey	25 A1

Rowerstown Lane 17 A3[3]
Royal Canal Bank 11 B2
Royal Canal Court 11 B2[13]
Royal Canal Tce 11 A3
Royse Road 11 B1
Russell Avenue 12 D2
Russell Ave East 13 B3
Russell Street 12 D2
Rutland Avenue 26 C3
Rutland Cottages 12 D3[4]
Rutland Place 12 C3
Rutland Place North 12 D3
Rutland St Lower 12 D3
Rutledge Terrace 26 D2
Ryder's Row 19 B1
Sackville Avenue 13 A2
Sackville Gardens 13 A2[1]
Sackville Place 20 C1
St. Agatha Court 13 A3[10]
St. Aidan's Park 6 C3
St. Aidan's Pk Ave 6 C3
St. Aidan's Pk Rd 14 C1
St. Alban's Street 27 A2
St. Alphonsus Ave 12 C1[1]
St. Alphonsus Rd Lwr 12 C1
St. Alphonsus Rd Upr 12 C1
St. Andrews Lane 20 C3[11]
St. Andrews Street 20 C3
St. Anne's Rd Nth 12 C1
St. Anne's Road Sth 26 D2
St. Anthony's Place 12 C3[1]
St. Anthony's Road 26 C1
St. Attracta Road 2 C3
St. Audoen's House 19 A2[5]
St. Audoen's Tce 19 B3[4]
St. Augustine Street 19 A2
St. Barnaba's Gdns 13 B2
St. Benedict's Gdns 12 C2[4]
St. Brendan's Cotts 22 D3
St. Brendan's Road 12 C1
St. Bricin's Park 18 C1
St. Brigid's Avenue 13 B2
St. Brigid's Drive 7 B1
St. Brigid's Cotts 13 B2[9]
St. Brigid's Court 7 B1
St. Brigid's Gardens 21 B1
St. Brigid's Road 8 C1
St. Brigid's Rd Upr 12 C1
St. Catherine's Ave 26 D2
St. Catherine's La W 19 A3
St. Clare's Avenue 27 A3
St. Clement's Road 12 C1[2]
St. Columba's Rd Lwr 12 C1
St. Columba's Rd Upr 12 C1
St. David's Court 15 B1[5]
St. David's Terrace 10 C3
(Blackhorse Ave)

St. David's Terrace 3 B1
(Glasnevin)
St. Declan's Road 6 C3
St. Declan's Terrace 6 C3
St. Eithne Road 10 D1
St. Elizabeth's Ct 10 D2
St. Finbar's Road 2 C3
St. Finbarr's Court 1 B3[1]
St. Fintan Road 10 D1
St. Fintan Terrace 2 D3
St. Francis Square 19 B3[1]
St. George's Ave 12 D1
St. Helena's Road 1 B1
St. Ignatius Avenue 12 C2
St. Ignatius Road 12 C1
St. Ita's Road 3 B2[1]
St. James's Avenue 12 C1
St. James's Avenue 18 C3
St. James's Terrace 26 C2
(Dolphins Barn)
St. James' Terrace 31 A1[1]
(Sandymount)
St. James's Walk 26 C1
St. Jarlath Road 10 D1
St. John's Avenue 19 A3[5]
St. John's Cottages 17 B3[2]
St. John's Court 6 D2[1]
St. John's Rd West 17 B2
St. John's Street 27 A1[1]
St. John's Terrace 17 B3[12]
St. John's Wood 15 B1[2]
St. Joseph's Avenue 13 A1
(Clonliffe Road)
St. Joseph's Avenue 12 C1
(Drumcondra)
St. Joseph's Cotts 13 A3[13]
St. Joseph's Court 10 D3[2]
St. Joseph's Mansions 13 A3
St. Joseph's Parade 11 B2
St. Joseph's Place 11 B3[8]
(Phibsborough)
St. Joseph's Place 10 D3
(Prussia Street)
St. Joseph's Road 10 D3
St. Joseph's Square 16 D2[2]
St. Joseph's Street 12 C2[7]
St. Joseph's Terrace 12 D2[13]
(North Circular Rd)
St. Joseph's Tce 13 B1[3]
(Marino)
St. Joseph's Tce 22 D3[12]
(Ringsend)
St. Joseph's Villas 13 A2[9]
St. Kevin's Cotts 27 B2[1]
St. Kevin's Parade 27 B2
St. Kevin's Road 27 B3

St. Laurence Place 11 B3[2]
St. Laurence Pl E 21 B1[1]
St. Lawrence Road 15 A1
St. Lawrence's Court 7 A3
St. Laurence's Gdns 21 A1
St. Maignenn's Tce 17 B3[6]
St. Malachy Road 4 C2
St. Margaret's Ave 19 A3[6]
(Pimlico)
St. Margaret's Ave 26 D1[1]
(Cork Street)
St. Margaret's Ave N 12 D2[11]
St. Margarets Tce 26 D1
St. Mary's Ave Nth 11 B3[6]
St. Mary's Lane 29 B1[5]
St. Mary's Mansions 12 D3[10]
St. Mary's Place Nth 11 B3
St. Mary's Rd Nth 14 C3
St. Mary's Rd Sth 29 B2
St. Mary's Terrace 18 D1[3]
(Arbour Hill)
St. Mary's Terrace 11 B3
(Phibsborough)
St. Mary's Terrace 22 D3[14]
(Ringsend)
St. Michael's Close 19 B3[10]
St. Michael's Hill 19 B3[8]
St. Michael's Place 11 B3[15]
St. Michael's Road 4 C2
St. Michael's Tce 27 A1
St. Michan's House 19 B2[6]
St. Michan's Lane 19 B2[7]
St. Michan's Street 19 B2
St. Mobhi Boithrin 3 B1
St. Mobhi Court 3 B1
St. Mobhi Drive 3 B2
St. Mobhi Grove 3 B2
St. Mobhi Road 3 B2
St. Mura's Terrace 13 B3[2]
St. Nicholas Place 19 B3
St. Patrick's Avenue 13 B2[3]
St. Patrick's Close 27 B1
St. Patrick's Parade 12 C1
St. Patrick's Place 11 B3[1]
St. Patrick's Road 12 C1
St. Patrick's Terrace 12 D1[2]
(Fitzroy Ave)
St. Patrick's Terrace 12 D2[9]
(Russell St)
St. Patrick's Villas 22 D3
St. Paul Street 19 A1
St. Peter's Avenue 11 A2
St. Peter's Court 11 B2[4]
St. Peter's Road 11 A2
St. Philomena's Rd 3 A3
St. Stephen's Gn E 28 D1

St. Stephen's Gn N	20	D3
St. Stephen's Gn S	28	C1
St. Stephen's Gn W	28	C1
St. Teresa Place	3	B3
St. Teresa Road	3	B3
St. Teresa's Gdns	26	D2
St. Thomas Road	27	A1
St. Ultan's Flats	28	C2[6]
St. Vincent's Court	6	C1[1]
St. Vincent St Nth	11	B2[10]
St. Vincent St Sth	27	B2
Sampson's Lane	20	C1
Sandford Avenue	26	D2
Sandford Gardens	27	A2
Sandford Park	27	A2[2]
Sandwith St Lwr	21	A2
Sandwith St Upr	21	A3
Sandymount	31	A2
Sandymount Ave	30	D3
Sandymount Castle	31	A2[3]
Sandymount Cas Dr	31	A2
Sandymount Cas Pk	31	B2
Sandymount Cas Rd	31	A2
Sandymount Court	31	A1[2]
Sandymount Green	31	A2[2]
Sandymount Road	31	A1
Sarah Place	17	A2
Sarsfield Street	11	B2[11]
Sarsfield Quay	18	D2
School Street	18	D3
Schoolhouse Lane	20	D3
Schoolhouse La W	19	B3[3]
Seafield Avenue	16	D1
Seafield Court	16	C1[1]
Seafield Road East	16	D1
Seafield Road West	16	C1
Seafort Avenue	31	A2
Seafort Cottages	31	A2
Seafort Gardens	31	A1
Seafort Terrace	31	A2[1]
Seafort Villas	31	A2
Sean MacDermott St Lower	12	D3
Sean MacDermott St Upper	12	D2
Sean O'Casey Ave	12	D3
Sean Moore Road	23	A3
Seapoint Terrace	22	D3[15]
Seaview Ave E	14	C3
Seaveiw Ave Nth	15	A1
Second Avenue	21	B1
Selskar Terrace	28	D3
Serpentine Avenue	30	D3
Serpentine Park	30	D2
Serpentine Road	30	D2
Serpentine Terrace	30	D2
Seven Oaks	5	A1
Seville Place	12	B1/13 A3
Seville Terrace	13	A3
Shamrock Cottages	13	A3[3]
Shamrock Place	13	A3[2]
Shamrock Street	11	B3
Shamrock Terrace	13	A3
Shandon Crescent	10	D1
Shandon Drive	11	A1
Shandon Gardens	2	D3
Shandon Park	11	A1
Shandon Road	11	A1
Shanganagh Road	4	C3
Shannon Terrace	17	B3[5]
Shaw Street	20	D2
Shaw's Lane	30	C1
Shelbourne Avenue	30	C2
Shelbourne Lane	30	C2[1]
Shelbourne Road	30	C1
Shellysbanks Road	24	C3
Shelmalier Road	14	C3
Shelmartin Avenue	5	B3
Shelmartin Terrace	5	B3
Sheriff Street Lower	21	A1
Sheriff Street Upper	21	B1
Sherkin Gardens	4	D1
Sherrard Avenue	12	C2
Sherrard Court	12	C2[6]
Sherrard St Lwr	12	D2
Sherrard St Upr	12	C2
Ship Street Great	19	B3
Ship Street Little	19	B3
Shrewsbury	31	A3
Sibthorpe Lane	29	A3
Sigurd Road	18	D1
Simmon's Place	12	D3[2]
Simmonscourt Road	30	D3
Simpson's Lane	22	D3[16]
Sion Hill Court	5	B1
Sion Hill Road	5	B1
Sir John Rogerson's Qy	21	B2
Sitric Place	18	D1[1]
Sitric Road	18	D1
Skreen Road	9	A2
Slade Row	18	C1
Slane Road	25	B3
Slaney Close	2	C2
Slaney Road	2	C2
Slemish Road	9	A2
Slievenamon Road	25	A1
Smithfield	19	A2
Smithfield Terrace	19	A1[5]
Somerset Street	22	C3
South Circular Rd (Dolphin's Barn)	26	C2
South Circular Rd (Islandbridge)	17	A2
South Circular Rd (Kilmainham)	25	B1
South Bank Road	23	B3
South Dock Place	22	C3
South Dock Road	22	C3
South Dock Street	22	C3
South Link Road	31	A1
South Lotts Road	22	C3
Spa Road	9	A3
Spafield Terrace	30	D3[3]
Spencer Avenue	21	B1
Spencer Place	13	B2[11]
Spencer Row	20	D1[3]
Spencer St North	13	B2
Spencer St South	27	B2
Spencer Terrace	26	D1[3]
Spitalfields	19	A3[11]
Spring Avenue	13	A2
Spring Garden La	20	D2
Spring Garden St	13	A2
Springfield (Glasnevin)	9	A2
Springfield	3	B1
Stable Lane (Leeson Street)	28	D1
Stable Lane (Arran Qy)	19	A2
Stable Lane (Harcourt St)	28	C1
Stamer Street	27	B2
Stanhope Street	19	A1[2]
Stanley Street	19	A1
Steeven's Lane	18	C2
Stella Avenue	4	C1
Stella Gardens	22	D3
Stephen Street Lower	20	C3
Stephen Street Upper	19	B3
Stephen's Lane	29	A1
Stephens Place	29	A1
Stephens Road	25	A1
Stirrup Lane	19	A1
Stoke's Place	28	C1
Stoney Road	13	B2
Stoneybatter	18	D1
Store Street	20	D1
Strand Road	31	B2
Strand Street	23	A3
Strand Street Great	19	B2
Strand Street Little	19	B2
Strandville Avenue	13	B2
Strandville Ave E	15	A1[4]
Strandville Ave E	14	D1
Strandville House	15	A1[1]
Strandville Place	13	B2[8]
Strangford Gardens	13	B3
Strangford Rd East	13	B3

Strasburg Terrace	22 D3[8]	
Strongs Court	20 C1[2]	
Suffolk Street	20 C2	
Suir Road	25 A1	
Sullivan Street	17 B1[1]	
Summer Arch	12 D2	
Summer Place	12 D3	
Summer St North	12 D3	
Summer St South	18 D3	
Summerhill	12 D3	
Summerhill Parade	13 A2	
Summerhill Place	12 D3	
Summerville	16 C2	
Sundrive Road	25 B3	
Susan Terrace	27 A1	
Susanville Road	13 A1	
Sussex Road	29 A2	
Sussex Terrace	28 D2[3]	
Swan Alley	19 A3	
Swan Grove	28 D3	
Swan Place	29 A3	
Sweeney's Terrace	27 A1	
Swift's Alley	19 A3	
Swift's Row	20 C2	
Swilly Road	9 B1	
Sword Street	18 C1	
Swords Road	5 A1	
Sybil Hill Road	8 D2	
Sycamore Street	20 C2	
Sydenham Road	30 D3	
Synge Lane	27 B2	
Synge Place	28 C2	
Synge Street	28 C2	
Synnott Place	12 C2	
Synnott Row	12 C2[8]	
Taaffe's Place	13 B2	
Talbot Lane	20 D1[7]	
Talbot Place	20 D1	
Talbot Street	20 D1	
Tangier Lane	20 C3[15]	
Tara Street	20 D2	
Taylor's Lane	18 D3	
Temple Bar	20 C2	
Temple Buildings	11 B3[10]	
Temple Cottages	11 B3	
Temple Court	18 C1	
Temple Lane North	12 C3	
Temple Lane South	20 C2	
Temple Place	28 D3	
Temple Street West	18 C1	
Temple Villas	18 C1[3]	
Terminal Rd Nth	24 D1	
Terminal Rd Sth	24 D1	
Terrace Place	12 D3[5]	
The Appian Way	29 A3	
The Bramblings	7 B2	
The Court	15 A1	
The Crescent	5 A1	
The Grove	5 A1	
The Haven	3 B1	
The Meadows	8 D1	
The Mews	15 B1	
The Orchard	8 C1	
The Pines	8 C1	
The Square	22 D3	
The Stiles Road	7 B3	
The Sweepstakes	30 C2[27]	
The Turrets	30 D2	
The Village	4 D1	
The Willows	2 D2	
Third Avenue	21 B1	
Thomas Court	18 D3	
Thomas Davis St Sth	19 A3	
Thomas St West	18 D3	
Thomas Lane	20 C1	
Thompson's Cotts	12 D3[3]	
Thor Place	18 C1[1]	
Thorncastle Street	22 D2	
Thorndale Drive	7 A1	
Thorndale Grove	7 A1	
Thundercut Alley	19 A1	
Tolka Cottages	2 D1	
Tolka Estate Road	2 D1	
Tolka Quay Road	23 A1	
Tolka Road	13 A1	
Tolka Valley Road	1 A1	
Tom Kelly Road	28 C2	
Tom Clarke House	13 A1[1]	
Torlogh Gardens	13 B1	
Torlogh Parade	5 B2[2]	
Tower View Cotts	3 A3	
Townsend Street	20 D2	
Traynor Place	17 B3[13]	
Trinity Place	21 A2[4]	
Trinity Street	20 C2	
Trinity Terrace	13 A2[13]	
Tritonville Avenue	31 A1	
Tritonville Close	31 A1[3]	
Tritonville Court	31 A2	
Tritonville Crescent	31 A1	
Tritonville Road	30 D1	
Turvey Avenue	17 A3[2]	
Tyrrel's Lane	22 D3[9]	
Tyrrell Place	12 D2[15]	
Ulster Street	11 A1	
Ulster Terrace	13 A2[5]	
Upper Cross Road	25 B1	
Usher Street	19 A2	
Usher's Island	18 D2	
Usher's Lane	19 A2[8]	
Usher's Quay	19 A2	
Valentia Parade	12 C2	
Valentia Road	4 C1	
Vauxhall Avenue	26 C1	
Vavasour Square	30 C1	
Venetian Hall	8 C1	
Ventry Drive	1 A3	
Ventry Park	1 A3	
Ventry Road	1 B3	
Vera Terrace	4 C2[2]	
Vernon Street	27 B1	
Vernon Avenue	8 C2/16 D	
Vernon Court (Clontarf Road)	16 D2	
Vernon Court (Seafield Road)	16 D1	
Vernon Drive	8 D2	
Vernon Gardens	16 D1	
Vernon Grove	16 D1	
Vernon Heath	8 D3	
Vernon Park	8 D3	
Vernon Rise	8 D2	
Veronica Terrace	22 D3[6]	
Verschoyle Court	29 B1	
Verschoyle Place	29 A1	
Vicar Street	19 A3	
Victoria Cottages	22 D3[13]	
Victoria Lane	4 D3	
Victoria Quay	18 D2	
Victoria Road	15 B1	
Victoria Street	27 B2	
Victoria Villas	6 D3	
Viking Harbour	18 D2[3]	
Viking Place	18 D1	
Viking Road	18 D1	
Violet Hill Drive	2 D1	
Violet Hill Park	2 D1	
Violet Hill Road	2 D1	
Walker's Cottages	28 C3	
Walker's Court	28 C3[7]	
Walnut Avenue	4 D1	
Walnut Lawn	4 D1	
Walnut Park	4 D1	
Walnut Rise	4 D1	
Walsh Road	4 C2	
Walworth Street	27 B2[5]	
Ward's Hill	27 A1	
Warner's Lane	28 D2	
Warren Street	27 B2	
Warrenmount	27 A1[9]	
Warrenmount Place	27 A1[2]	
Warrenpoint	15 B1[1]	
Warrington Lane	29 B1	
Warrington Place	29 B1	
Warwick Terrace	29 A3[1]	
Washington Street	27 A2	
Waterfall Avenue	5 A3	
Waterloo Avenue	13 B2	

Waterloo Lane   29 A3
Waterloo Road   29 A3
Watkin's Buildings   27 A1⁶
Watling Street   18 D2
Waverley Avenue   13 B1
Weaver Lane   11 B2⁶
Weaver's Close   27 A1⁷
Weaver's Street   27A1
Weaver's Square   27 A1¹⁰
Wellesley Place   12 D2¹⁰
Wellington Lane   29 B3
Wellington Place   29 B3
Wellington Pl Nth   11 B3⁴
Wellington Quay   20 C2
Wellington Road   29 B2
Wellington Road   17 A2
 (Phoenix Park)
Wellington St Lwr   11 B3
Wellington St Upr   11 B3
Wellpark Avenue   4 D1
Werburgh Street   19 B3
Wesley Place   27 A2
West Road   13 B3
Western Road   26 D2
Western Way   11 B3
Westland Row   21 A3
Westmoreland St   20 C2
Wexford Street   28 C1
Whelan House   22 D3¹⁰
Whitebank Road   23 B3
Whitefriar Gardens   19 B3¹³
Whitefriar Place   20 C3⁹
Whitefriar Street   19 B3
Whitehall   5 A1
Whites Lane North   11 B3¹¹
Whitworth Avenue   12 D2²
Whitowrth Parade   12 C1⁴
Whitworth Place   12 C1³
Whitworth Road   11 B1
Whitworth Terrace   12 D1³
Wicklow Street   20 C3
Widow's Houses   19 A3²⁰
Wigan Road   11 B1
Wilfield   31 A3
Wilfield Park   31 A3
Wilfield Road   31 A3
Willbrook House   28 D3⁶
William St Nth   13 A2
William St Sth   20 C3
William's Lane   20 C1
William's Pl Lwr   12 D2⁴
William's Place Sth   27 B1
Williams Pl Upr   12 C2⁵
Willie Bermingham Pl   17 B3¹
Willowfield   31 B3
Wilson Terrace   19 A3

Wilson's Terrace   21 A3¹
Wilton Court   29 A2¹
Wilton Place   29 A2
Wilton Terrace   29 A2
Windele Road   4 C2
Windmill Lane   21 A2
Windmill Road   25 A3
Windsor Avenue   13 B1
Windsor Place   28 D1
Windsor Terrace   27 B3
Windsor Villas   13 B1²
Winetavern Street   19 B2
Winton Road   29 A3
Wolfe Tone Quay   18 C2
Wolfe Tone Street   19 B1
Wolseley Street   27 A2³
Wood Lane   18 D2¹
Wood Quay   19 B2
Wood Street   19 B3
Woodville Road   4 C3¹
Wormwood Gate   19 A2⁷
Xavier Road   19 B2
Yarnhall Street   19 B1²
York Road   22 D2
York Street   28 C1
Zardoz Court   30 C3⁴
Zoo Road   17 A1

LIST OF STREETS
NOT NAMED ON MAP
AND SHOWN BY
SMALL NUMBERS

      Grid
Page Ref.   Street Name

1   B3 1 St. Finbarr's Court
2   D1 1 Bellevue Cottages
2   D3 1 Coke Ovens Cotts
3   B2 1 St. Ita's Road
4   C2 1 O'Neachtain Road
        2 Vera Terrace
4   C3 1 Woodville Road
4   D2 1 Beaucourt
4   D3 1 Edgewood
        2 Clonturk Gardens
        3 Ivetta Terrace
5   B2 1 Morrogh Road
        2 Torlogh Parade
6   C2 1 St. Vincent's Court
6   D2 1 St. John's Court
        2 Cherrymount Grove
        3 Cherrymount Cres
7   B2 1 Quarry Cottages
8   D3 1 Duncan Court
9   A2 1 Parkview Court
10 C3 1 Ashford Place
        2 Ashford Cottages

10 D1 1 Fertullagh Road
10 D3 1 Aughrim Villas
        2 St. Joseph's Court
        3 Kings Court
        4 Aughrim Court
11 A1 1 Connaught Parade
11 A2 1 Castle Terrace
11 A3 1 Orchard View
        2 Grangegorman Villas
11 B2 1 Library View Tce
        2 Cowley Place Upper
        3 Cowley Place Lwr
        4 St. Peter's Court
        5 Lynch's Place
        6 Weaver Lane
        7 Kelly's Lane
        8 Phibsborough Place
        9 Aranmore Avenue
       10 St. Vincent St Nth
       11 Sarsfield Street
       12 Bective Square
       13 Royal Canal Court
       14 George's Wharf
11 B3 1 St. Patrick's Place
        2 St. Laurence Place
        3 Primrose Street
        4 Wellington Pl Nth
        5 Graham's Row
        6 St. Mary's Ave Nth
        7 Blessington Court
        8 St. Joseph's Place
        9 Mountjoy St Middle
       10 Temple Buildings
       11 White's Lane North
       12 Broadstone Avenue
       13 Kings Inns Court
       14 Mauncell Place
       15 St. Michael's Place
       16 Delvin Terrace
12 C1 1 St. Alphonsus Ave
        2 St. Clement's Road
        3 Whitworth Place
        4 Whitworth Parade
12 C2 1 Kenmare Parade
        2 Muckross Parade
        3 Derrynane Parade
        4 St. Benedict's Gdns
        5 Williams Place Upr
        6 Sherrard Court
        7 St. Joseph's Street
        8 Synnott Row
        9 De Velara Place
       10 Josephine Avenue
       11 Leo Avenue
       12 George's Place

12 C3 1 St. Anthony's Place
2 Hardwicke Arch
3 Hardwicke Lane
4 Frederick Court
5 Gardiner Row
6 Hardwicke Place
7 Frederick Lane Nth
8 Bethesda Place
9 Cavendish Row
10 Britain Place
12 D1 1 Robert Place
2 St. Patrick's Terrace
(FitzroyAve)
3 Whitworth Terrace
12 D2 1 Drumcondra Park
2 Whitworth Avenue
3 Portland Court
4 William's Place Lwr
5 Belvidere Avenue
6 Campbell's Lane
7 Campbell's Row
8 Portland Square
9 St. Patrick's Tce
(RussellSt)
10 Wellesley Place
11 St. Margaret's Ave Nth
12 Richmond Lane
13 St. Joseph's Tce
(N.C.Rd)
14 Mountjoy Parade
15 Tyrrell's Place
16 Brenden Behan Ct
12 D3 1 Matt Talbot Court
2 Simmon's Place
3 Thompson's Cotts
4 Rutland Cottages
5 Terrace Place
6 Bella Place
7 Bella Avenue
8 Gloucester Lane
9 Gloucester Pl Lwr
10 St. Mary's Mansions
11 Liberty House
12 Buckingham Village
13 Gloucester Diamond
14 Lourdes House
15 Langrishe Place
16 Belmont Place
17 Father Scully House
18 Mountain View Ct
19 Avondale House
13 A1 1 Tom Clarke House
13 A2 1 Sackville Gardens
2 Richmond Crescent
3 Richmond Cottages
4 Clonmore Villas

5 Ulster Terrace
6 Clinch's Court
7 Newcomen Court
8 Charlemont Parade
9 St. Joseph's Villas
10 Richmond Parade
11 Foster Place North
12 Ballybough Lane
13 Trinity Terrace
14 Ballybough Court
15 Ballybough Avenue
16 King's Avenue
17 Catherine Court
13 A3 1 Guildford Place
2 Shamrock Place
3 Shamrock Cottages
4 Duke Row
5 Portland Close
6 Buckingham Place
7 Killarney Avenue
8 Preston Street
9 Beaver Close
10 St. Agatha Court
11 Halpin's Row
12 Aldborough Square
13 St. Joseph's Cotts
13 B1 1 Caragh Court
2 Windsor Villas
3 St. Joseph's Tce
(Marino)
13 B2 1 Courtney Place
2 Annesley Avenue
3 St. Patrick's Avenue
4 Poplar Row (Apts)
5 Leinster Street East
6 James's Street Nth
7 Northbrook Terrace
8 Strandville Place
9 St. Brigid's Cotts
10 Austin's Cottages
11 Spencer Place
13 B3 1 Malachi Place
2 St. Mura's Terrace
14 C3 1 Boolavogue Road
14 D1 1 Crescent House
15 A1 1 Strandville House
2 Hollybrook Ct Drive
3 Hollybrook Court
4 Strandville Ave East
15 B1 1 Warrenpoint
2 St. John's Wood
3 Knightsbridge
4 Lambourne Village
5 St. David's Court
15 B2 1 Alverno
2 Haddon Court

16 C1 1 Seafield Court
16 D2 1 Churchgate Avenue
2 St. Joseph's Square
17 A2 1 Park Place
2 Islandbridge Court
3 Hospital Lane
17 A3 1 Rosemount Court
2 Turvey Avenue
3 Rowerstown Lane
4 Kearn's Place
5 Carrickfoyle Terrace
6 Prospect Terrace
7 Millbrook Terrace
8 Ashmount Court
17 B1 1 Sullivan Street
2 Black Street
17 B3 1 Willie Bermingham Pl
2 St. John's Cottages
3 Irwin Court
4 Irwin Street
5 Shannon Terrace
6 St. Maignenn's Tce
7 Owens Avenue
8 Almeida Avenue
9 Ceannt Fort
10 Auburn Terrace
11 Knocknarow Tce
12 St. John's Terrace
13 Traynor Place
14 Lorne Terrace
15 Mill Brook
16 Camac Terrace
18 C1 1 Thor Place
2 Montpelier Gardens
3 Temple Villas
18 C2 1 De Burgh Road
2 Park Avenue West
18 C3 1 McDowell Avenue
2 Kilmainham Village
3 Prior Hall
4 Mary Aikenhead Ho
18 D1 1 Houghton Terrace
2 Sitric Place
3 St. Mary's Tce
(ArbourHill)
18 D2 1 Wood Lane
2 Hendrick Place
3 Viking Harbour
4 John's Street North
5 Hendrick Lane
6 Ellis Court
18 D3 1 Rainsford Avenue
2 Marshalsea Lane
3 Marrowbone La Bldg

19 A1	1	Fitzwilliam Pl Nth
	2	Stanhope Street
	3	Catherine Lane Nth
	4	Father Matthew Sq
	5	Smithfield Terrace
	6	Marmion Court
	7	Friary Grove
	8	Kevin Barry Flats
19 A2	1	Burgess Lane
	2	Coke Lane
	3	Lincoln Lane
	4	Morgan Place
	5	St. Audoen's House
	6	Oliver Bond House
	7	Wormwood Gate
	8	Usher's Lane
	9	Mullinahack
19 A3	1	Brabazon Square
	2	Gray Square
	3	Meath Square
	4	Reginald Square
	5	St. John's Avenue
	6	St. Margaret's Ave
	7	Brabazon Street
	8	Coombe Court
	9	Hanover Street W
	10	Park Terrace
	11	Spitalfields
	12	Liberty Square
	13	Meath Market
	14	Ash Grove
	15	Crostick Alley
	16	Flag Alley
	17	Engine Alley
	18	Pimlico Cottages
	19	Poole Street
	20	Widow's Houses
19 B1	1	Lurgan Street
	2	Yarnhall Street
	3	Constitution Hill (Flats)
	4	Linenhall Street
	5	Henrietta House
19 B2	1	Essex Gate
	2	Exchange St Lwr
	3	Meetinghouse Lane
	4	Ormond Place
	5	Hamilton Court
	6	St. Michan's House
	7	St. Michan's Lane
	8	Cork Hill
19 B3	1	St. Francis Square
	2	Davis Place
	3	Schoolhouse La W
	4	St. Audoen's Terrace
	5	Borris Court
	6	John Field Road
	7	Longford St Great
	8	St. Michael's Hill
	9	Christchurch Sq
	10	St. Michael's Close
	11	Iveagh Bldgs (BrideSt)
	12	Lord Edward Court
	13	Whitefriar Gardens
	14	Hanover Court
	15	Power's Square
	16	Clarence Mangan Sq
	17	Bride Close
20 C1	1	Findlater Place
	2	Strongs Court
20 C2	1	Litton Lane
	2	Abbey Cottages
	3	Adair Lane
	4	Bedford Row
	5	Asdill's Row
	6	Merchants Arch
	7	Fownes Street Lwr
	8	Cecilia Street
	9	Crampton Court
	10	Parliament Row
	11	Champion Quay
	12	Palace Street
20 C3	1	Harry Street
	2	Chatham Lane
	3	Balfe Street
	4	Coppinger Row
	5	Chatham Row
	6	Clarendon Market
	7	Longford Street Little
	8	Longford Lane
	9	Whitefriar Place
	10	Glendinning Lane
	11	St. Andrews Lane
	12	Johnson Place
	13	Clarendon Row
	14	Chatham Row
	15	Tangier Lane
	16	Glovers Court
20 D1	1	Frenchman's Lane
	2	Moland Place
	3	Spencer Row
	4	Marlborough Place
	5	Northumberland Sq
	6	Deverell Place
	7	Talbot Lane
20 D2	1	Corn Exchange Pl
	2	Rath Row
	3	Bracken's Lane
	4	Brunswick Villas
	5	Cards Lane
	6	Leinster Market
20 D3	1	Nassau Place
	2	Molesworth Place
	3	Kildare Place
21 A2	1	Magennis Square
	2	Peterson's Court
	3	Lombard Court
	4	Trinity Square
	5	Countess Markievicz Ho
21 A3	1	Wilson's Terrace
	2	Merrion Close
	3	Cumberland Court
	4	College Lane
21 B1	1	St. Laurence Pl East
	2	Blythe Avenue
	3	Ferrymans Crossing
	4	Bellman's Walk
21 B3	1	Island Villa
	2	Greenore Terrace
	3	Rostrevor Terrace
	4	Pearse Grove
	5	Clanwilliam Square
	6	Clanwilliam Terrace
	7	Hogan Place
	8	Albert Place East
	9	Conway Court
22 C1	1	Carbury Terrace
	2	Irvine Cottages
	3	Church Place
	4	Church Avenue
	5	Church Row
22 C3	1	Ormeau Street
22 D2	1	Fisherman's Wharf
22 D3	1	Cambridge Court
	2	Canon Mooney Gdns
	3	Parkview Place
	4	Herbert Place
	5	Philomena Terrace
	6	Veronica Terrace
	7	Magdalen Terrace
	8	Strasburg Terrace
	9	Tyrrel's Place
	10	Whelan House
	11	O'Rahilly House
	12	St. Joseph's Tce
	13	Victoria Cottages
	14	St. Mary's Terrace (Ringsend)
	15	Seapoint Terrace
	16	Simpson's Lane
	17	George Reynolds Flats
23 A3	1	Kyle-Clare Road
25 A1	1	Hybreasal
25 B1	1	Almeida Terrace
25 B3	1	Moracrete Cottages
26 C1	1	McCarthy Terrace
	2	Colbert's Fort
	3	Fatima Mansions
	4	Rialto Place

	5	Boardman's Lane
26 D1	1	St. Margaret's Ave
	2	Huxley Crescent
	3	Spencer Terrace
	4	Brandon Terrace
	5	Marrowbone Lane Close
	6	Our Lady's Close
26 D2	1	Priestfield Cottages
	2	Priestfield Drive
	3	Ellford Terrace
27 A1	1	St. John's Street
	2	Warrenmount Place
	3	Geoffrey Keating Rd
	4	Cow Parlour
	5	O'Curry Avenue
	6	Watkin's Buildings
	7	Weaver's Close
	8	Brabazon Place
	9	Warrenmount
	10	Weaver's Square
27 A2	1	Greenville Parade
	2	Sandford Park
	3	Wolseley Street
	4	Brainsboro Terrace
	5	Griffith Square
	6	Garden Terrace
	7	Greenville
27 A3	1	Hatters Lane
	2	Greenmount Square
	3	Armstrong Street
	4	Le Vere Terrace
	5	Harold's Cross Cotts
27 B1	1	Old Mill Court
	2	St. Kevins Avenue
	3	Iveagh Buildings (Kevin St. Upr)
	4	Malpas Court
	5	Cathedral View Walk
	6	Church Lane South
	7	Harry Court
	8	Cross Kevin Street
	9	New Street Gardens
	10	Long Lane Close
27 B2	1	St. Kevin's Cottages
	2	Rosedale Terrace
	3	Kingsland Pk Ave
	4	Florence Street
	5	Walworth Street
	6	Bloomfield Cottages
	7	Janeville
27 B3	1	Greenfield Place
	2	Fitzgerald Street
	3	Ashworth Place
	4	Drummond Place
	5	Grove Avenue
28 C1	1	Aungier Lane
	2	Protestant Row
	3	Montague Court
	4	O'Neill's Buildings
	5	Camden Villas
	6	Camden Buildings
28 C2	1	Camden Court
	2	Camden Street Old
	3	Camden Market
	4	Richmond Villas
	5	Gordon Place
	6	St. Ultan's Flats
	7	Charlemont Gdns
	8	French Mullen Flats
	9	Richmond Place S
	10	Harcourt Lane
	11	Albert Terrace
	12	Lennox Terrace
	13	Portobello Place
	14	Charlemont Place
28 C3	1	Observatory Lane
	2	Lissenfield
	3	Cheltenham Place
	4	Bannaville
	5	Garden View
	6	Mountpleasant Pde
	7	Walker's Court
	8	Mountpleasant Tce Upr
28 D1	1	Fitzwilliam Court
	2	Ely Place Upper
	3	Mackie's Place
28 D2	1	Convent Place
	2	Pembroke Place
	3	Sussex Terrace
28 D3	1	Dexter Terrace
	2	Mountpleasant Pl
	3	Mander's Terrace
	4	Mountpleasant Villas
	5	Crosbie House
	6	Willbrook House
	7	Cullen's Wood
	8	Osbourne Tce
29 A1	1	Convent Close
	2	Baggotrath Place
	3	Fitzwilliam Pl Little
29 A2	1	Wilton Court
29 A3	1	Warwick Terrace
	2	Berystede
	3	Mitchell House
29 B1	1	Cranmer Lane
	2	Love Lane East
	3	Grattan Ct East
	4	Mount St Cres
	5	St. Mary's Lane
	6	Clanwilliam Court
	7	Grattan Hall
	8	Bridge Court
29 B2	1	Eastmoreland Pl
29 B3	1	Morehampton Sq
	2	Morehampton Mews
	3	Ardoyne House
	4	Hampton Court
30 C1	1	Lansdowne Tce
	2	Emerald Cotts
	3	Lansdowne Villas
	4	Lansdowne Cres
	5	Berkeley Mews
30 C2	1	Shelbourne Lane
	2	Lansdowne Gdns
	3	Carlton Villas
	4	Herbert Cotts
	5	Dodder View Cotts
	6	Estate Cottages
	7	The Sweepstakes
30 C3	1	Ballsbridge Tce
	2	Pembroke Pl (Ballsbridge)
	3	Granite Place
	4	Zardoz Court
30 D1	1	Havelock Terrace
	2	Lansdowne Hall
	3	Barrack Lane
30 D2	1	Railway Cottages
	2	Martin White Chalets
	3	Homelee
	4	Claremont Court
30 D3	1	Prince of Wales Tce
	2	Lynton Court
	3	Spafield Terrace
	4	Adair
	5	Churchill Terrace
	6	Ballsbridge Park
31 A1	1	St. James's Tce
	2	Sandymount Ct
	3	Tritonville Close
	4	Prospect Terrace
31 A2	1	Seafort Terrace
	2	Sandymount Grn
	3	Sandymount Cas
31 B2	1	Hepenstal Tce
31 B3	1	Bethany House